westermann

Dirk Aßmann, Irene Hartwig-Hannemann, Thomas Meinen, Brigitte Nies

Store and More

Alles auf Lager. Englisch

3. Auflage

Bestellnummer 225330

Die in diesem Produkt gemachten Angaben zu Unternehmen (Namen, Internet- und E-Mail-Adressen, Handelsregistereintragungen, Bankverbindungen, Steuer-, Telefon- und Faxnummern und alle weiteren Angaben) sind i. d. R. fiktiv, d. h., sie stehen in keinem Zusammenhang mit einem real existierenden Unternehmen in der dargestellten oder einer ähnlichen Form. Dies gilt auch für alle Kunden, Lieferanten und sonstigen Geschäftspartner der Unternehmen wie z. B. Kreditinstitute, Versicherungsunternehmen und andere Dienstleistungsunternehmen. Ausschließlich zum Zwecke der Authentizität werden die Namen real existierender Unternehmen und z. B. im Fall von Kreditinstituten auch deren IBANs und BICs verwendet.

Zusatzmaterialien zu „Store and More"

Für Lehrerinnen und Lehrer

        Lösungen zum Arbeitsbuch: 978-3-14-225334-3
        Lösungen zum Arbeitsbuch Download: 978-3-14-225332-9

Zu diesem Produkt sind digitale Zusatzmaterialien kostenlos online für Sie erhältlich. Sie können diese ganz einfach über die Eingabe des nachfolgenden Codes im Suchfeld unter www.westermann.de abrufen.

BVE-225330-001

Sollten Sie zu diesem Produkt bereits eine BiBox mit Material erworben haben, so sind die Zusatzmaterialien selbstverständlich dort bereits integriert.

© 2023 Westermann Berufliche Bildung GmbH, Ettore-Bugatti-Straße 6-14, 51149 Köln
www.westermann.de

Das Werk und seine Teile sind urheberrechtlich geschützt. Jede Nutzung in anderen als den gesetzlich zugelassenen bzw. vertraglich zugestandenen Fällen bedarf der vorherigen schriftlichen Einwilligung des Verlages. Nähere Informationen zur vertraglich gestatteten Anzahl von Kopien finden Sie auf www.schulbuchkopie.de.

Für Verweise (Links) auf Internet-Adressen gilt folgender Haftungshinweis: Trotz sorgfältiger inhaltlicher Kontrolle wird die Haftung für die Inhalte der externen Seiten ausgeschlossen. Für den Inhalt dieser externen Seiten sind ausschließlich deren Betreiber verantwortlich. Sollten Sie daher auf kostenpflichtige, illegale oder anstößige Inhalte treffen, so bedauern wir dies ausdrücklich und bitten Sie, uns umgehend per E-Mail davon in Kenntnis zu setzen, damit beim Nachdruck der Verweis gelöscht wird.

> **Die Seiten dieses Arbeitshefts bestehen zu 100 % aus Altpapier.**
>
> Damit tragen wir dazu bei, dass Wald geschützt wird, Ressourcen geschont werden und der Einsatz von Chemikalien reduziert wird. Die Produktion eines Klassensatzes unserer Arbeitshefte aus reinem Altpapier spart durchschnittlich 12 Kilogramm Holz und 178 Liter Wasser, sie vermeidet 7 Kilogramm Abfall und reduziert den Ausstoß von Kohlendioxid im Vergleich zu einem Klassensatz aus Frischfaserpapier. Unser Recyclingpapier ist nach den Richtlinien des Blauen Engels zertifiziert.

Druck und Bindung: Westermann Druck GmbH, Georg-Westermann-Allee 66, 38104 Braunschweig

ISBN 978-3-14-**225330**-5

VORWORT

Das Englischbuch „Store and More" ist Teil der Reihe „Alles auf Lager". In fünf Units werden wesentliche Themenschwerpunkte aus dem Berufsalltag von Fachlageristen und Fachkräften für Lagerlogistik behandelt.

„Store and More" ist ein Lehr- und Arbeitsbuch, das den Schülerinnen und Schülern die Möglichkeit bietet, einen Großteil der Lösungen direkt in das Buch einzutragen. Diese Arbeitsweise erleichtert die Nachbereitung des Erlernten sowie die Vorbereitung auf Klassenarbeiten und Prüfungen. Die Inhalte des Buches orientieren sich am KMK-Rahmenlehrplan für die Ausbildung zur Fachlageristin bzw. zum Fachlageristen und zur Fachkraft für Lagerlogistik sowie an den bundeslandbezogenen Lehrplänen für Englisch an berufsbildenden Schulen. Berufsbezogene Texte und praxisnahe Übungen dienen als handlungsorientiertes Training für alle wichtigen Lernebenen, Hör- und Leseverstehen sowie Sprachproduktion, Interaktion und Mediation. Das spezifische Fachvokabular wird in abwechslungsreichen Aufgabenstellungen eingeführt und geübt.

Jede Unit enthält wesentliche Bestandteile, die dem Buch eine klare und verständliche Struktur verleihen:

- Grammar boxes: Die Einheiten bestehen jeweils aus einer übersichtlichen Darstellung der wichtigsten Regeln der englischen Grammatik und darauf aufbauenden Übungen mit steigendem Schwierigkeitsgrad.
- Word banks: Zum Verständnis der Hör- und Lesetexte sowie zur Bearbeitung der Übungen ist schwieriges Vokabular in übersichtlich gestalteten Kästen aufgeführt.
- Tips and skills: Wertvolle Hinweise wie *How to start a presentation* oder *Appropriate style in business correspondence* dienen der Weiterentwicklung der Methodenkompetenz und erinnern an Besonderheiten der englischen Sprache.
- Business correspondence: Alle grundlegenden Formen der Geschäftskommunikation wie *Telephoning, E-Mails* und *Business letters* werden der Zielgruppe angemessen behandelt.

In einem umfangreichen Anhang können die Vokabeln nach Units gegliedert oder alphabetisch geordnet schnell nachgeschlagen werden. Die von Muttersprachlern gesprochenen Hörtexte können über den Webcode im Impressum dieses Buches auf www.westermann.de abgerufen werden. Der Schwierigkeitsgrad der Texte und Übungen ist gemäß dem Gemeinsamen Europäischen Referenzrahmen für Sprachen auf der Niveaustufe A2/B1 einzuordnen.

Autoren und Verlag wünschen viel Erfolg bei der Arbeit mit dem Buch. Anregungen und Hinweise sind jederzeit willkommen.

Word List: Word Banks	Topics	
1 My Business	1.1 Meeting People	7
	1.2 Inside the Company	10
	1.3 Business Correspondence	19
2 Warehouse Safety	2.1 Dangers at Work	30
	2.2 Safety Issues	33
	2.3 Health and Safety Hazards	40
	2.4 Safety Signs and Safety Clothing	43
	2.5 Business Correspondence	46
3 Receiving and Storing Goods	3.1 Receiving Goods	55
	3.2 Registration of Goods Receipt	60
	3.3 Storing Goods	64
	3.4 Correct Storage	66
	3.5 Storage Systems	68
	3.6 Hazardous Goods	70
	3.7 Business Correspondence	71
4 Order Picking and Packing Goods	4.1 Order Picking	82
	4.2 Packing Goods	87
	4.3 Business Correspondence	99
5 Transport and Logistics	5.1 European Countries	108
	5.2 Organising a Transport	110
	5.3 Going Global	112
	5.4 Modes of Transport	116
	5.5 Material Handling Equipment for Internal Transport	121
	5.6 Documents in National and International Trade	124
	5.7 Innovations in Warehousing and Logistics	126
	5.8 Business Correspondence	131
Appendix	Phonetic Alphabet	
	Word Banks	
	Alphabetical Word List	
	Irregular Verbs	
	Summary of English Tenses	
	Picture Credits	

CONTENTS

Page	Grammar		Tips & Skills		Communication & Correspondence	
6	The Verb "to be"	9	How to Start a Presentation	9	Telephoning	19
	Present Simple	13	There is/There are	17		
	Present Perfect	17				
	Present Continuous	21				
29	Simple Past	37	Charts, Graphs and Statistics	32	E-Mails and Business Letters	46
	Pronouns	42	Mediation	36		
			Appropriate Style in Business Correspondence	50		
54	Will-Future	59	Professional Presentations	55	Enquiries	71
	If-Clauses, Type I	62	Listening for Gist	56		
	Countable and Uncountable Nouns	77	Internet Research	64		
			Letter of Enquiry	76		
81	Word Order	95	How to Hold a Presentation	89	Orders	99
	Adjectives and Adverbs	97				
107	Comparison of Adjectives	115	Capitalisation in Written English	107	Complaints and Apologies	131
	Passive Voice	119	How to Write a Discussion	114		
			Method "Think-Pair-Share"	128		
			Project Based Learning (PBL)	130		
138						
139						
146						
161						
164						
165						

1 My Business

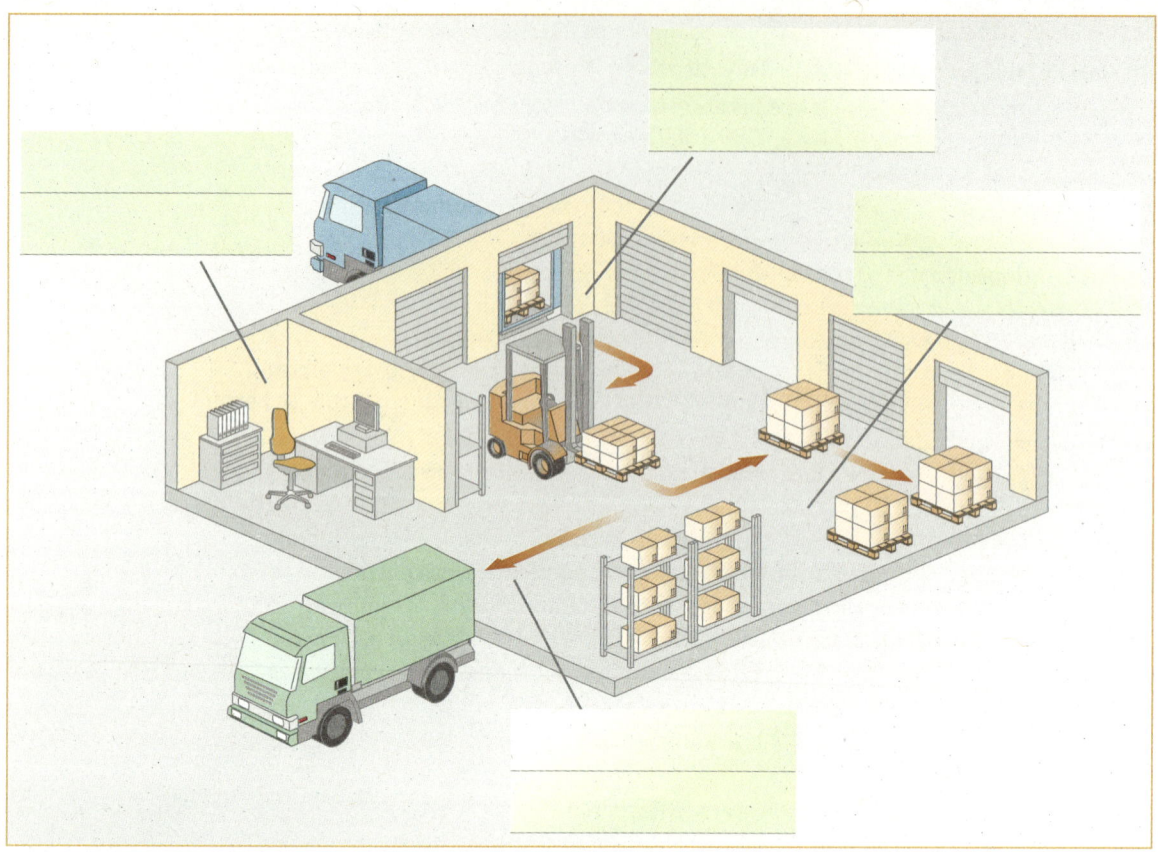

MATCHING

Look at the floor plan above and label the different warehouse areas with the correct terms from the box.

goods receipt | goods dispatch | stock | warehouse administration

DISCUSSION

a. Talk with a partner and make notes about his/her company and his/her workplace. Use the following prompts:
- how did he/she find his/her apprenticeship?
- warehouse area he/she works in
- company's name
- location
- number of employees
- goods stored

b. Now present your findings about your partner to the class.

> **TIP** You can start your presentation like this:
> – My partner's name is …
> – He/She works in …
> – He/She found the …

My Business

1.1 Meeting People

1.1.1 LISTENING

Listen to the conversation on Brian's first day in his new job and complete the missing parts in the text below.

Steve: Come in!
Brian: Good morning.
Steve: Good morning. _____ I help you?

Brian: Yes, sir. My name is Brian Stone, I'm the _____ .

Steve: Oh yes, Brian, _____ . I'm Steve, Steve Askins, the warehouse supervisor. I think first of all I'll show you around and _____ you to your other colleagues.

Brian: That would be _____ .

Steve: Okay, this way _____ .
Brian: Thank you.
Steve: Hello Robert, _____ Brian, our _____ .

Robert: _____ you, Brian.

Brian: Hello, nice to _____ .

Robert: We are quite busy today. A lot of goods _____ and have to be stored and registered in the system. The guy over there _____ is Allan. He is the one you will be working with.

Brian: I see.
Steve: I'll show Brian around _____ , so he can get an idea of his new _____ . I guess we'll be back within half an hour.

Then you can introduce him _____ .
Robert: Okay, see you later then.

WORD BANK		
	apprenticeship	Ausbildungsplatz
	employee	Mitarbeiter/-in
	goods issue	Warenausgang
	goods receipt	Wareneingang
	location	Standort
	stock	Lager
	warehouse administration	Lagerverwaltung
	warehouse operator	Fachlagerist/-in
	warehouse supervisor	Lagerleiter/-in
	workplace	Arbeitsplatz

My Business

1.1.2 MATCHING

Put the following dialogue between Sarah and David into the correct order.

[1.] Good morning. I'm Sarah Martin, the new apprentice.

[ ] Thanks, nice to meet you.

[ ] No, it's only ten miles away from Bristol.

[ ] Yes, I come by bus.

[ ] Oh, it's only a twenty-minute bus ride.

[ ] No, I'm not from Bristol. I am from Clutton.

[ ] So, it doesn't take too long?

[ ] Nice to meet you, too. Are you from Bristol?

[ ] How do you get to work? Do you come by bus?

[ ] I see, from Clutton. That's about 15 miles away from Bristol, isn't it?

[ ] Good morning, I'm David White. Please, call me David, we are not so formal around here.

[ ] And how long does it take to get here?

1.1.3 ROLE PLAY

Act out the following situation with a partner.

Ute Cremer holt Sandy Fisher am Empfang ab. Es ist der erste Tag in der Firma für Sandy Fisher.

Ute Cremer begrüßt Sandy Fisher und fragt, ob sie die neue Kollegin ist.	→	Sandy Fisher bejaht die Frage und begrüßt Ute Cremer ebenfalls.
Sie stellt sich vor und heißt Sandy Fisher herzlich willkommen bei Futuristic Logistics Ltd.	→	Sandy Fisher findet das nett und bedankt sich.
Sie möchte Sandy ihr Büro zeigen und bittet sie, ihr zu folgen.	→	Sie bedankt sich.

My Business

TIP

Useful language

Hello/Hi,	my name is Dorothea Pale. I'm Susan Bright.	May I introduce you to … This is ……
I'm	the new employee. the new colleague. the supervisor.	I'll show you round the warehouse. That would be nice. This way, please.
Please call me Susan. We are not so formal here.		Nice to meet you. Nice to meet you, too Welcome to ……

HOW TO USE

The Verb "to be"

Positive Aussagen		Verneinung		Frage
I **am**	I'm	I **am not**	I'm **not**	**Am** I …?
you **are**	you're	you **are not**	you're **not**	**Are** you …?
he/she/it **is**	he's, she's, it's	he/she/it **is not**	he's **not**, she's **not**, it's **not**	**Is** he/she/it …?
we/you/they **are**	we're, you're, they're	we/you/they **are not**	we're **not**, you're **not**, they're **not**	**Are** we/you/they …?

1.1.4 EXERCISE

Fill in the correct form of the verb "to be".

Brian: Hi Sarah, (1) _____ you from London?

Sarah: No, I (2) _____ from London, I'm from Liverpool. – And you, Brian, where (3) _____ you from?

Brian: I'm from London – do you know London?

Sarah: Only a little, but I know it (4) _____ nice there. Do you like the city?

Brian: Yes, I like London. It (5) _____ a great place. Many tourists visit the city every year, because there (6) _____ a lot of sights and a lot of things to do in the city.

Sarah: What (7) _____ your favourite place or sight in London?

Brian: Oh, that (8) _____ difficult to say. There (9) _____ a lot of interesting sights. For instance, there is the famous Buckingham Palace, the Tower of London and Big Ben. But there (10) _____ high entrance fees.

1 My Business

1.2 Inside the Company

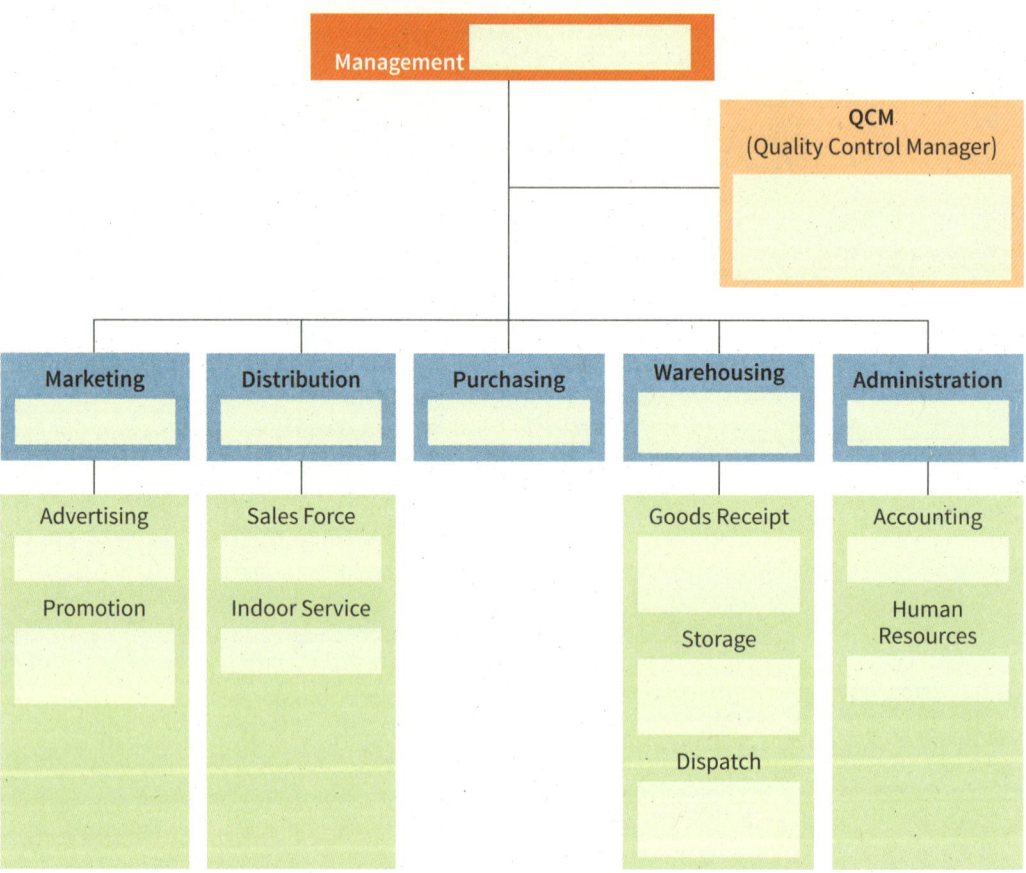

Organisation of *NextGeneration Food Ltd.*

1.2.1 TRANSLATION

Find the German translations for the different departments of this company by using a dictionary.

1.2.2 ANALYSING

Refer to the organisational chart above and answer the following questions in complete sentences.

1. If a customer wants to order something, which department does he/she contact?

2. Which department should interested candidates send their job application to?

3. Which department is in charge of placing orders?

   _____

4. What is the responsibility of the marketing department?

   _____

5. By which department are the goods shipped to the customers?

   _____

1.2.3 VOCABULARY WORK

Complete the company profile below with the words from the box.

> business | distributes | farmers | needs | purchase | retail | success | team | warehouse | wholesaler

A Company Profile

NextGeneration Food Ltd. is a large (1) _____ of health food and organic food. The company (2) _____ a wide range of groceries to supermarkets, retail stores, restaurants and a large number of catering companies. It is a privately held company based in Tetbury. Operating all over the United Kingdom, a flexible distribution network helps to serve the customers' (3) _____.

We (4) _____ high quality goods direct from selected manufacturers and (5) _____. Organic and naturally produced, healthy food is our mission as well as locally produced food. Our modern (6) _____ with high-tech storage equipment and processing technology makes us among the best in the food distribution sector. As part of our (7) _____ concept, we provide customised service to our (8) _____ customers. We give our business partners great support and resources in terms of marketing techniques but also in logistics and technical issues.

The entire (9) _____ at NextGeneration Food Ltd. consists of experienced staff. These dedicated workers represent a key source of our (10) _____.

My Business

1.2.4 ANALYSING

Answer the following questions on the text above in complete sentences.

1. What does *NextGeneration Food Ltd.* distribute?

2. Who are the company's customers?

3. Where do the products come from?

4. What services does *NextGeneration Food Ltd.* provide to its customers?

1.2.5 WRITING

Write a similar profile of the company you work for or a company you know.

WORD BANK		
	customised	kundenspezifisch
	dedicated	engagiert
	groceries	Lebensmittel
	organic food	Biolebensmittel
	to provide with	versorgen mit
	to purchase	(ein)kaufen
	staff	Belegschaft, Mitarbeiter
	resource	Mittel
	retail	Einzelhandel
	success	Erfolg
	support	Unterstützung
	wholesaler	Großhändler

My Business

HOW TO USE

Present Simple	
Anwendung:	
1. wenn etwas immer wieder passiert oder etwas immer so ist, Signalwörter: always, never, usually, sometimes, often etc.	I **work** for Futuristic Logistics.
2. wenn etwas im Fahrplan oder im Programm angegeben ist	He **watches** TV every night.
3. wenn man Gefühle, Gedanken, Meinungen ausdrückt	Robert **loves** his girlfriend.
Bildung:	

Positive Aussage	Verneinung	Frage
I/you work	I/you don't work	Do I/you work?
he/she/it works	he/she/it doesn't work	Does he/she/it work?
we/you/they work	we/you/they don't work	Do we/you/they work?

Achtung:
– bei der 3. Person Singular (he/she/it) wird ein „s" an den Infinitiv des Verbs gehängt
– endet das Verb auf einen Zischlaut, wird „**es**" angehängt, z.B. miss – miss**es**, watch – watch**es**; endet es auf „y", wird dieses zum „i", wenn der Buchstabe davor kein Vokal ist, z.B. carry – carr**ies**

1.2.6 EXERCISE

Put the verbs in brackets into the right form.

Example: *NextGeneration Food Ltd.* _____ (produce) healthy food.

1. We _____ (provide) customised service.
2. The team at *NextGeneration Food Ltd.* _____ (consist) of experienced staff.
3. Our business partners _____ (enjoy) great support.
4. Our modern technology _____ (make) us among the best in the business.
5. *NextGeneration Food Ltd.* _____ (give) great support to customers.

1.2.7 EXERCISE

Form negatives and questions out of the following sentences.

Example: The company distributes a wide range of groceries to supermarkets.
The company doesn't distribute a wide range of groceries to supermarkets.
Does the company distribute a wide range of groceries to supermarkets?

1. The company has its headquarters in Tetbury.

_____

My Business

2. *NextGeneration Food Ltd.* operates all over the United Kingdom.

3. We purchase the goods directly from selected manufacturers.

4. Our modern warehouse technology makes us among the best in the business.

5. We provide customised service to our retail customers.

1.2.8 LISTENING FOR GIST

a. Listen to three people talking about their jobs at *NextGeneration Food Ltd.* and complete the table below.

	Steven McPhery	Jennifer Humphry	Rosa Garcia
… works in which department?			
… has been with the company for how long?			
… finds his/her job …			

My Business

b. Listen again and complete the following sentences.

1. I (1) _____ the goods in stock.
2. Different types of goods (2) _____ and handled in a different way, depending on their nature.
3. Keeping the (3) _____ up to date is my job, too.
4. I (4) _____ in this position (5) _____ last September and I like my work here at *NextGeneration Food Ltd.*
5. (6) _____ and maintaining a good relationship with our customers is the (7) _____ of my job.
6. My job (8) _____ is to increase the (9) _____ of orders.
7. It is a very (10) _____ and I don't know how long I will be able to do it.
8. I have been with *NextGeneration Food Ltd.* (11) _____.
9. Today, (12) _____ two candidates for a vacancy in the purchasing department.
10. If we come to an agreement, we will sign an (13) _____.
11. Apart from hiring new staff, I also organise (14) _____.

1.2.9 READING

a. Read the text about *NextGeneration Food Ltd.* to understand the main facts.

History of *NextGeneration Food Ltd.*

The company started as a small distributor of local vegetables and fruit in 1998. The owner and founder, John Montell, established the company in the basement of a former factory in Chippenham. The idea of locally grown and healthy products was a success and soon after its humble beginnings the company had grown a lot. At that time, the company consisted of 15 employees.

When John Montell decided to add organic food to his range of products in 2002, the company was rapidly faced with a shortage of storage capacity which in turn led to the relocation of the warehouse to Tetbury in 2003. A year later, in 2004, a new office building adjacent to the warehouse in Tetbury was inaugurated. The distribution service which had started with a radius of 80 miles had accelerated to a distribution network all over the United Kingdom.

The way John Montell managed the company and its staff contributed to the continuing growth of the company; it had become a flourishing business and its staff had increased to a considerable number of around 350 employees.

My Business

2015 was the year John Montell retired and his son Ryan Montell, together with his wife Susan Montell-Swenson, took over. The new management team expanded their services, by adding packaged and canned as well as frozen organic food to their product line. This brought further growth of the company. Today, the company has five branches all over the United Kingdom. It is still family owned and employs some 1,200 people.

b. Read the text for a second time and underline all the numbers in the text in order to complete the time line below.

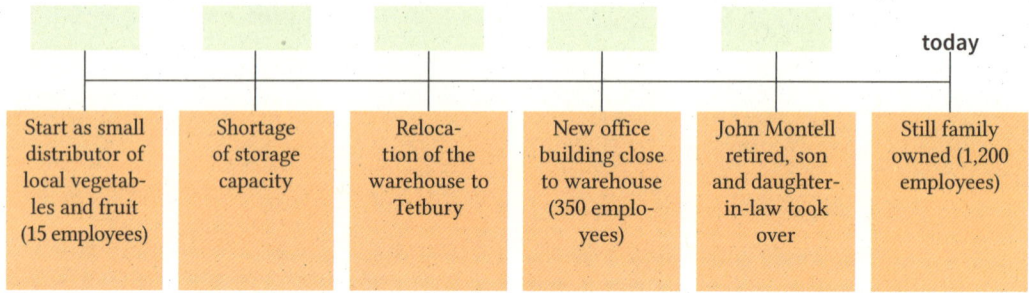

						today
Start as small distributor of local vegetables and fruit (15 employees)	Shortage of storage capacity	Relocation of the warehouse to Tetbury	New office building close to warehouse (350 employees)	John Montell retired, son and daughter-in-law took over	Still family owned (1,200 employees)	

c. With the help of the timeline give a short account of the company history of *NextGeneration Food Ltd*.

WORD BANK

to accelerate	zunehmen	humble	bescheiden
founder	Gründer	in turn	wiederum
considerable	beträchtlich, beachtlich	to inaugurate	einweihen
to establish	errichten, gründen	owner	Eigentümer/-in
to expand	expandieren, erweitern	product line	Sortiment
factory	Fabrik	relocation	Umzug/Verlegung
to flourish	florieren	shortage	Engpass
growth	Wachstum	to take over	übernehmen

My Business

	Vocabulary „es" in Verbindung mit einer Form von „to be" wird durch „there" wiedergegeben: there is / there are: es gibt, es ist / es sind, es befindet sich / es befinden sich		
TIP	there is / there's	There is no doubt that he is the boss.	Es besteht kein Zweifel, dass ...
	there are / there're	There are many mistakes in this business letter.	Es befinden sich ...
	Is there ...?	Is there an elevator?	Gibt es ...?
	Are there ...?	Are there enough goggles?	Gibt es ...?

HOW TO USE

Present Perfect	
Anwendung:	
1. wenn eine Handlung gerade stattgefunden hat oder ein Vorgang eine Beziehung zur Gegenwart hat, Signalwörter: just, already, ever, never, up to now, (not) yet	I **have** just **phoned** my colleague. I **have** never **been** to America.
2. wenn ein Vorgang in der Gegenwart noch andauert, Signalwörter: since (für Zeitpunkt in der Vergangenheit), for (für Zeitspanne)	I **have been** with the company for two years. I **have been** with the company since 2010.
3. wenn ein Vorgang in der Vergangenheit stattgefunden hat, aber der Zeitraum nicht genannt wird	He **has visited** London. I **have met** a famous person.
4. wenn der Zeitraum, über den gesprochen wird, noch andauert, Signalwörter: this week, today	The company **has grown** a lot this year.
Bildung: Present Perfect = has/have + past participle (Verb + "-ed" oder 3. Form des Verbs)	

Positive Aussage	Verneinung	Frage
I/you **have** arriv**ed**	I/you **haven't** arriv**ed**	**Have** I/you arriv**ed**?
he/she/it **has** arriv**ed**	he/she/it **hasn't** arriv**ed**	**Has** he/she/it arriv**ed**?
we/you/they **have** arriv**ed**	we/you/they **haven't** arriv**ed**	**Have** we/you/they arriv**ed**?

1.2.10 EXERCISE

Complete the following sentences by using the correct form of the verb in brackets.

1. We (1) _____ (deliver) high-quality products to customers all over the world since 2010.

2. Our staff (2) _____ (learn) a lot in the computer course.

3. I (3) _____ (never be) to our subsidiary in Australia.

4. Look, my colleague (4) _____ (buy) a new car.

My Business

5. They (5) _____ (not yet dispatch) the ordered goods.

6. The manager _____ (not yet agree) to a pay rise.

7. The company _____ (become) the market leader in organic food.

8. *NextGeneration Food Ltd.* _____ (sell) this product since May.

1.2.11 TRANSLATION

Translate the following sentences into English.

1. Ich arbeite seit drei Monaten bei der Firma.

2. *NextGeneration Food Ltd.* ist Marktführer für Biolebensmittel geworden.

3. Die Lieferung ist gerade angekommen.

4. Die Verkäufe sind in den letzten zwei Jahren deutlich gestiegen.

5. Tim hat die Waren bereits gepackt.

6. Der Manager hat der Installation des neuen Systems zugestimmt.

7. Ich war noch niemals in Edinburgh.

8. Unsere Firma hat in diesem Jahr zwei neue Autos gekauft.

My Business

1.3 Business Correspondence – Telephoning

1.3.1 READING

a. Adam McKinsey, the manager of the Edinburgh branch of *NextGeneration Food Ltd.*, has received the following e-mail. Complete the e-mail by using the prepositions from the box below.

by | for | in | of | to | with

From	r.taylor@ngf.co.uk
To	a.mckinsey@ngf-edinburgh.co.uk
Date	10 October 20..
Subject	Visit to Edinburgh branch

Dear Adam

As discussed earlier, the management is planning to improve the performance of the order picking system (1) _____ the Edinburgh warehouse. For this purpose I am arranging a visit together (2) _____ our Director Ryan Montell and a software engineer (3) _____ EasyStore at your site. Would 9 August 20.. be convenient (4) _____ you to show us round? We will come (5) _____ train to Waverley Station and would need a transfer (6) _____ the warehouse.
Please let me know if that will be okay with you.

Regards
Robin

From	a.mckinsey@ngf-edinburgh.co.uk
To	r.taylor@ngf.co.uk
Date	10 October 20..
Subject	Visit to Edinburgh branch

Dear Robin
I'm very sorry but we can't make it on 9 August as a number of staff, including me, are going to a full day training course. Would a week later be okay for you? I will be available any day except Tuesday.

Regards
Adam

My Business

b. **Adam McKinsey answered the e-mail on the same day. Read his reply on page 19 and answer the following questions.**

1. Why does Adam not agree to the visit on 9 August?

2. What is his suggestion?

1.3.2 LISTENING FOR DETAIL

A day later, Adam receives a phone call from Robin. Listen to the conversation twice and try to fill in the missing words.

Adam: *NextGeneration Food Ltd.*, Adam McKinsey speaking, how can I help you?
Robin: Hi Adam, this is Robin. How are you doing?
Adam: I'm fine, thanks — a little bit tied up with work, but (1) _____ smoothly. And you?

Robin: I'm fine, too. (2) _____ about Mr Montell's visit to Edinburgh concerning the installation of a new order picking system.
Adam: Yes, Robin. It's about arranging a date for the visit.
Robin: Right. The problem is that Mr Montell's schedule is very tight. This is why (3) _____ to arrange a date with you. You suggested the week after 9 August. Mr Montell (4) _____ with an important customer on Monday and the engineer is not available, either, he (5) _____ another company on Wednesday. So we've only got Thursday and Friday.
Adam: That's great for me. I'm only tied up on Tuesday.
Robin: So, let's fix it for Thursday then. Can you pick us up at Waverley at 10 o'clock?

Adam: Mmh, (6) _____ a briefing at 9:30 – but I think I can manage to be at Waverley at 10 o'clock.
Robin: Okay, fine. I'll arrange everything for our visit to your site.

Adam: All right, (7) _____ forward to seeing you.
Robin: Me, too. See you then. Bye.
Adam: Bye.

My Business

HOW TO USE

Present Continuous	
Anwendung:	
1. wenn etwas gerade im Augenblick des Sprechens passiert, Signalwörter: now, at the moment, right now etc.	I **am** do**ing** my homework at the moment.
2. wenn etwas in der Zukunft fest geplant ist	He **is** fly**ing** to China next Monday.
3. wenn jemand etwas ausnahmsweise tut	Normally, I work in Hamburg, but today I **am** work**ing** in Munich.
4. wenn etwas zeitlich begrenzt ist	Brian **is** work**ing** at the company during the summer.
Bildung:		
Positive Aussage	Verneinung	Frage
I **am** read**ing**	I **am not** read**ing**	**Am** I read**ing**?
you **are** read**ing**	you **are not** read**ing**	**Are** you read**ing**?
he/she/it **is** read**ing**	he/she/it **is not** read**ing**	**Is** he/she/it read**ing**?
we/you/they **are** read**ing**	we/you/they **are not** read**ing**	**Are** we/you/they read**ing**?
Achtung: – endet der Infinitiv auf "e", so entfällt dieses, z.B. make – making – nach einem kurzen Vokal wird ein Konsonant am Ende des Verbs verdoppelt, z.B. cut – cutting		

1.3.3 EXERCISE

Present Simple or Present Continuous? Put in the verbs in the right forms.

1. Look! Betty (1) _____ (go) to her car.

2. Ms Cohen (2) _____ (walk) to work at 7:30 every morning.

3. The bus usually (3) _____ (stop) in front of the factory.

4. Mr Summer is busy, he (4) _____ (write) an e-mail.

5. The manager (5) _____ (visit) the branch next Thursday.

6. The food in the canteen (6) _____ (taste) delicious.

7. Where are Charles and Bob? They (7) _____ (load) the lorry at the moment.

8. They usually (8) _____ (have) their lunch break from 12 o'clock to 1 o'clock.

1

My Business

1.3.4 EXERCISE

Some of the following sentences are right and some are wrong. Put a tick (✓) next to the right ones, and correct the wrong ones.

1. I am getting to work by bus every morning.

2. Ben works in the marketing department.

3. Mr Montell is on the phone, he is talking to the engineer.

4. The office is closed. The staff takes part in a time management course.

5. Next week, Allan is visiting the Manchester branch.

6. The warehouse is containing all the goods in stock.

7. Patrick is a student, he studies business administration at Dublin University.

8. He works at a pub during his summer holidays.

1.3.5 READING

The Manager's Visit

Mr Montell's visit is coming soon. The colleagues at the Edinburgh branch are busy arranging everything. Everything should **be in perfect order** when the manager comes to look around the warehouse. Even though he is only interested in improving the performance of the electronic picking system, the employees want to **make a good impression**. The warehouse staff are
5   cleaning and clearing up their workplaces and the office staff are trying to **bring** their records **up to date**. They are all **looking forward** eagerly to the boss's visit.

Adam McKinsey, the plant manager, is trying to book a hotel room for Mr Montell and his wife Susan Montell-Swenson as she has decided to **accompany** her husband at the last minute. After their visit to the warehouse, they want to stay a little longer in Edinburgh and **do some**
10 **sightseeing**.

My Business

It is quite complicated to find a suitable hotel for the couple because it is high season and lots of tourists are in town. The annual event of the Military Tattoo also takes place at Edinburgh Castle in August. This event attracts a large number of visitors from all over the globe.

Find expressions in the text that have the meaning of the following German terms:

1. sich freuen auf
2. in tadelloser Ordnung
3. einen guten Eindruck machen
4. Besichtigungen machen
5. etwas auf den neuesten/aktuellen Stand bringen
6. jemanden begleiten

1.3.6 WRITING

Make your own sentences using the expressions above.

WORD BANK		
	to arrange	ausmachen, arrangieren
	to be tied up	beschäftigt sein
	briefing	Einsatzbesprechung
	demanding	fordernd
	engineer	Techniker
	to look forward to doing sth.	sich darauf freuen, etwas zu tun
	to manage sth.	es schaffen, etwas zu tun
	schedule	Zeitplan
	smoothly	glatt, ohne Probleme
	to suggest	vorschlagen
	vacancy	offene Arbeitsstelle

My Business

1.3.7 LISTENING FOR GIST

Adam McKinsey has been on the phone all morning to find a hotel room for Mr and Mrs Montell. Listen to his phone call with the Castle Hotel and number the dialogue in the right order.

☐ Samantha: You're welcome, sir. Bye.

☐ Adam: Good morning, this is Adam McKinsey of *NextGeneration Food Ltd.* I would like to book a double room.

☐ Samantha: Certainly, sir. When would you like to stay?

☐ Adam: Oh, it's not for me, it's for our director and his wife. – They are arriving on Thursday, 18 August, and want to stay until Sunday, 20 August.

☐ Samantha: *Castle Hotel*, Samantha Grey speaking. Can I help you?

☐ Adam: No, Ms Grey, that wouldn't help. We definitely need a double room. Thank you for your help anyway. I think I'll try the Hilton. Maybe they have a double room left.

☐ Samantha: Just a second, Mr McKinsey, let me check the system. – I'm awfully sorry, but there is no double room available for that time. Due to the Military Tattoo, we are fully booked. There are only three single rooms left.

☐ Adam: Thank you, bye-bye.

HOW TO USE

Useful telephone language
Answering
Hello, Futuristic Logistics, Diana French speaking. Good morning.
Can I help you? What can I do for you?
Could you give me your name, please?
Can I have the invoice number/reference number?
All right, thank you, I'll put you through to the Accounts Department.
Hold the line please, I will try it once again.
I'm sorry, Mr Knight is not in his office.
Can I take a message? Would you like/do you want to leave a message?
Could Ms Simpson give you a call back/call you back?
Could you please give me your telephone number?
I'll repeat it: …
Thank you for calling.
Thanks/Thank you, have a nice day.
Calling
Good morning, my name is Allan Stone/this is Allan Stone/I'm Allan Stone of Fashion World.
I'd like to/Can I talk/speak to Mr Towen please?
Could you put me through to the Human Resources Department, please?
I'm calling about the consignment I received yesterday.
I'll try it again later/call again tomorrow.

My Business

1.3.8 SPELLING

The international telephone alphabet is very helpful when you have to spell complicated words, names, addresses etc. In this way, misunderstandings can be avoided when communicating with customers on the phone.

International Telephone Alphabet

A	like	Alpha		N	like	November
B	like	Bravo		O	like	Oscar
C	like	Charlie		P	like	Papa
D	like	Delta		Q	like	Quebec
E	like	Echo		R	like	Romeo
F	like	Foxtrot		S	like	Sierra
G	like	Golf		T	like	Tango
H	like	Hotel		U	like	Uniform
I	like	India		V	like	Victor
J	like	Juliet		W	like	Whisky
K	like	Kilo		X	like	X Ray
L	like	Lima		Y	like	Yankee
M	like	Mike		Z	like	Zulu

Note that it is also important to mention whether it is a capital letter or a small letter. Here are some useful punctuation marks for spelling out additional information.

WORD BANK

(…)	in brackets	-	dash
(	open bracket	_	underscore
)	close bracket	@	at
/	slash	.	dot in e-mails

Use the international telephone alphabet:
1. Take turns in spelling your own name.
2. Go back to page 19 and spell the e-mail addresses.
3. Take turns in writing a word on the board and ask a classmate to spell it out.

1.3.9 ROLE PLAY

a. With a partner, create a telephone conversation by using the activity cards. Write down the conversation.

My Business

b. Role play the dialogue.

① Vincent Marony	ACTIVITY CARD
You receive a phone call from *Futuristic Logistics*. They want to hire a lorry. Take down the following details:	

Customer name:

Phone number:

Date – from: to:

Method of Payment: in advance ☐   Credit card ☐

Prices per day:		Lorry No 1	Lorry No 2
	one day:	£ 140	£ 115
	three and more days:	£ 115	£ 95
	features:	box, 7.5 tons, tail lift	curtain, 7.5 tons

My Business

② Peter Sommer	ACTIVITY CARD

You work for *Futuristic Logistics*, Liverpool. Phone number: 0721-789866.

Your lorry has broken down. Call *Express CarRental* in order to hire a lorry. You need it immediately for five days. It has to be equipped with a tail lift. You will pay by credit card when you pick it up tomorrow.

c. Role play the dialogue.

① Patricia Newton	ACTIVITY CARD

Call the Ashton Hotel in London in order to book a hotel room for your boss, Mr Marco Barillo.

He is having a meeting with a business partner and wants to stay in London from 16 to 19 September. He needs Internet access and would prefer a balcony. Ask for the price of a suitable room. Mr Barillo will pay by credit card on arrival.

② Gordon Styles	ACTIVITY CARD

You are the receptionist at the Ashton Hotel in London.
Patricia Newton will call you. Take down the reservation.
You need the following details:

First Name:

Surname:

Date – from: – to:

Number of nights:

Prices per person per night	
Premium room	Orange room
Single £ 180	Single £ 175
Double £ 150	Double £ 130
Features: King Size Bed, Balcony, Internet Access	Features: King Size Bed, Internet Access

1 My Business

1.3.10 CROSSWORD PUZZLE

Find 12 hidden past participles in the grid and complete the table below. The first one has been done for you.

C	C	V	B	K	L	E	N	J	U	Z	Z
O	E	G	O	N	E	A	H	D	A	S	S
M	N	W	R	I	T	T	E	N	V	B	X
O	S	U	N	G	Z	E	L	G	B	M	Y
B	O	U	G	H	T	N	G	W	O	A	P
O	L	K	T	O	L	D	B	V	E	N	D
U	D	G	B	B	R	O	K	E	N	J	E
Q	V	N	G	F	I	N	T	Z	S	N	H
G	H	K	B	Z	B	E	C	O	M	E	X
N	O	T	T	F	R	I	G	Q	W	E	R

Infinitive	Past Simple	Past Participle	Deutsch (Infinitive)
go	went	gone	gehen

2 Warehouse Safety

DISCUSSION

The situations shown in the pictures above might look familiar to you. Daily work in the warehouse is full of surprises and dangerous situations. Describe the pictures above. Make up at least eight sentences. Feel free to use the words and phrases in the matching exercise.

MATCHING

Match the English words and phrases with their German equivalents.

☐ 1. workplace accident		a. einstürzen, zusammenfallen
☐ 2. to collapse		b. Lagerregal
☐ 3. forklift		c. Palette
☐ 4. to be injured		d. Arbeitsunfall
☐ 5. to load a lorry (BrE)/truck (AE)		e. Gabelstapler
☐ 6. storage rack		f. sich verletzen
☐ 7. pallet		g. einen Lkw beladen

2 Warehouse Safety

2.1 Dangers at Work

2.1.1 DISCUSSION

a. Work with your neighbour and tell him or her about critical situations you have experienced in your working life so far.
b. Complete the table below.

Dangers in the warehouse		
Dangerous or critical situations for warehouse staff	Reasons for warehouse accidents	Required actions by the employer

2.1.2 ANALYSING

In order to analyse the cartoon, follow these steps:

a. List the objects and people you see in the cartoon.

b. Describe the action taking place in the cartoon.

c. Choose from the statements below the one that expresses the message of the cartoon best. Explain your choice.

1. Safety at work is just a waste of time.
2. No matter how busy you are, safety always comes first.
3. Safety at the warehouse is a purely voluntary aspect.

2.1.3 DEALING WITH DATA AND STATISTICS

Use the sources below to work out the most common causes for forklift accidents and useful strategies to prevent fatalities. Look at the boxes below.

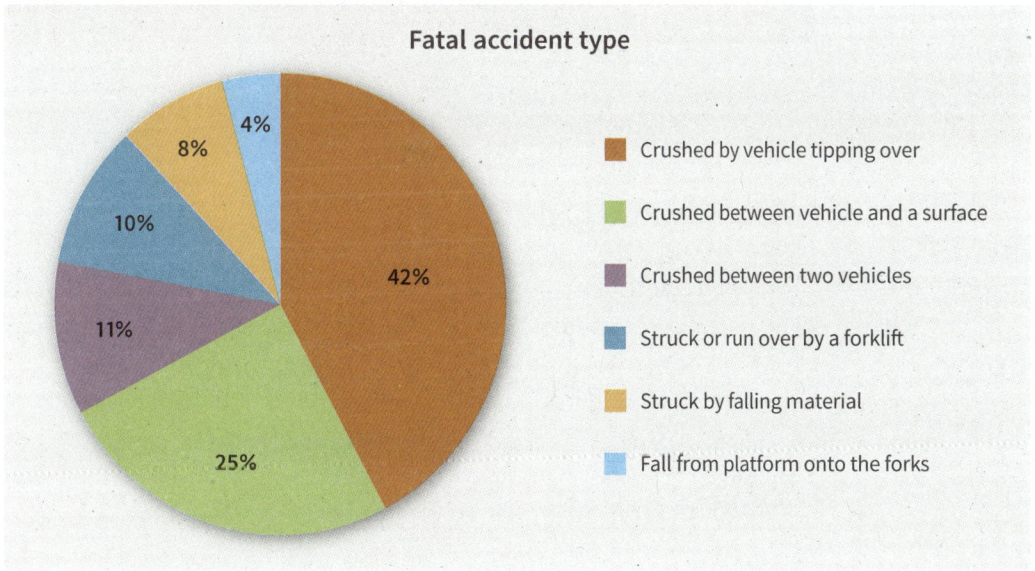

Chart 1: Fatal forklift accident causes

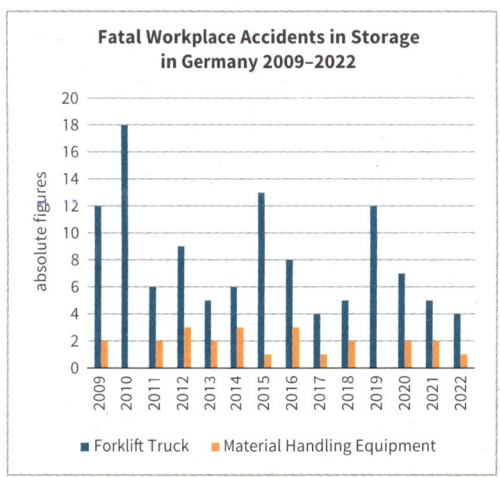

Charts 2 and 3: Fatal workplace accidents in business, industry and trade in Germany (Chart 2: figures taken from German Social Accident Insurance (DGUV): Statistics 2021. Figures and long-term trends, September 2022, Berlin, p. 44; Chart 3: figures taken from Bundesanstalt für Arbeitsschutz und Arbeitsmedizin, 2022, Dortmund)

Warehouse Safety

> **SKILLS**
>
> Charts, graphs or statistics can show complex information in a simple way. Follow these three steps:
> 1. Describe – Name general information such as title and source of the graph etc. and the date of publication.
> 2. Analyse – Dealing with figures and numbers. Point out the most remarkable and important numbers. Leave out less important information.
> 3. Evaluate – Try to find answers to the main questions, e. g. "Why is the Chinese economy so strong?" State your opinion and feel free to speculate.

HOW TO USE

Useful phrases for describing charts, graphs or statistics
The graph etc. shows …/compares …/illustrates …/reveals …
The graph shows how … has increased/has risen/has gone up/has grown in the last five years.
The statistics shows how … has decreased/has fallen/has gone down/has dropped in the last five years.
The outlook for … remains stable/steady/constant/at the same level etc.
Big changes can be expressed by "significant(ly)" or "substantial(ly)", small changes by "slight(ly)" or "little", fast changes by "sudden(ly)" or "sharp(ly)" and slow changes by "slow(ly)" or "gradual(ly)".

2.1.4 VOCABULARY

Read the following text and complete the gaps with the words in the box.

> accidents | back | dangerous | drivers | floor | head | neck | operate | prevent | rule | severity | vehicle

Preventing Fatal Forklift Accidents

Many of these (1) _____ could have been prevented by better training. No one starts out with the knowledge, skills, and abilities to safely

(2) _____ a forklift. Drivers must be properly trained to do so.

Operating a forklift without training is (3) _____. It can even be fatal to you or other employees working in the area.

Warehouse Safety

Training can also (4) _____ or reduce the (5) _____ of an accident. Keep the load as low as possible to increase (6) _____ stability and to help prevent tip-over accidents. Even if (7) _____ ignore this (8) _____ and the vehicle tips over, injuries are usually minor if they stay with the vehicle instead of jumping off. The normal tendency is for a person to jump downward, so the driver lands on the (9) _____ or ground, usually directly into the path of the overhead guard. The most common result is a crush injury to the (10) _____, (11) _____ or (12) _____ where the overhead guard strikes the employee.

2.2 Safety Issues

2.2.1 DISCUSSION

Read the statements below. Mark your position on the scales. With a partner, explain your choices. Then carry out a class survey and discuss the results in class.

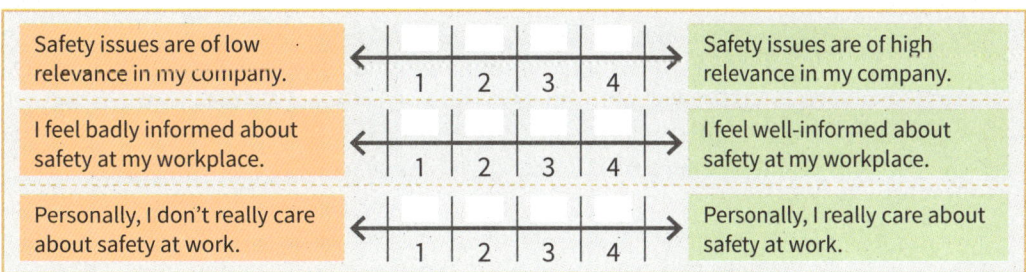

Safety issues are of low relevance in my company.	← 1 | 2 | 3 | 4 →	Safety issues are of high relevance in my company.
I feel badly informed about safety at my workplace.	← 1 | 2 | 3 | 4 →	I feel well-informed about safety at my workplace.
Personally, I don't really care about safety at work.	← 1 | 2 | 3 | 4 →	Personally, I really care about safety at work.

2.2.2 LISTENING

a. Listen carefully to the report "Dangers in the Warehouse" and answer the following questions below.

What are the two major threats in a warehouse?

_____

2 Warehouse Safety

Which other health and safety hazards in a warehouse should you keep in mind?

b. Referring to health and safety hazards in a warehouse, which of these are the most relevant ones? Explain your choice. Point out possible avoidance strategies.

2.2.3 READING

Read the text you have just listened to. With a partner, discuss why the statements on page 35 are true or false.

Dangers in the Warehouse

1 Paul has been working at his company for six months. He has **become familiar with** the work in the warehouse. Right from the start he learned all the things warehouse operators normally do and his colleagues have been a big help to him. Paul has now got a better understanding of the complex processes in a warehouse and the **hazards** that might **occur**. At the beginning he
5 was confronted with a huge number of laws and detailed instructions and regulations such as accident prevention regulations. His job includes a broad range of activities, for example using and operating a forklift, loading and unloading and storing goods.

One of the most important things everyone in his company has to consider is how to avoid situations that might lead to **severe injuries** or even **fatalities**. There are basically two main
10 **threats** to warehouse safety: in order to minimise fire hazards and to prevent accidents and injuries it is strictly **prohibited** to light a cigarette, to smoke or even to light a match. Flammable, explosive or chemical materials have to be stored in **fireproof** rooms. Fireproof doors should also be installed as well as fire exits and escape routes that lead to a safe place outside the building.

15 Last week, one of Paul's colleagues got fired because, over the last two years, he had stolen tools such as screwdrivers, pliers, electric drills, nails and screws. As a result of these **thefts** all workers at the warehouse had to take part in internal training with a special focus on 'Theft prevention in the warehouse'. The trainer explained that alarm systems, a clear storage system and regular checks would reduce the risk of theft significantly. Paul is surprised by the high
20 attention his new employer pays to safety. His former manager did not care much about safety in the warehouse. More than once wrong behaviour and a lack of safety standards led to dangerous situations.

Warehouse Safety

TRUE (=T) OR FALSE (=F)?

☐ 1. Paul does not get on very well with his colleagues because they ignore his problems.

☐ 2. Because of the risks, open fires are banned in a warehouse.

☐ 3. Laws and regulations of warehouse safety are for informational purposes only.

☐ 4. Paul's former employer had the same high safety standards as his current employer.

☐ 5. Fire exits and escape routes should be distinctively marked to avoid fatalities.

2.2.4 READING

After you have read the text carefully, answer the questions below the text in your own words. Do not copy whole passages from the text.

Warehouse Worker Injury Highlights Risk of Workplace Accidents

A worker at a textile retailer was injured after falling from a platform onto the concrete floor at the company's warehouse. The man had a broken leg and his ankle was crushed after a board had fallen onto it. He also received bad bruising to his face. The company had to pay
5 compensation after it was found that workers had no supervision or training and no protection against falling from heights of up to 30 feet. They had not been given specialist equipment and the ladders that were used were unsuitable and not fixed.

Falls from a height are one of the main causes of workplace accidents across all industries but the warehouse holds other dangers, too. Another worker was hit by a forklift truck. The
10 worker was kneeling down, measuring empty pallets when the truck ran over his right leg and hurt his foot. He broke three toes and fractured several bones in his foot. He had trouble walking for more than eighteen months after his accident.

Where vehicles and workers are in the same building there should be measures in place to ensure that both can move about separately and safely. Other hazards can include slips and
15 trips, manual lifting and the collapse of storage systems. Storage areas should be carefully planned and regularly inspected. Pallets or shelves should be loaded in a way that ensures stability and should not be overloaded.

Every year, there are more than 10,000 workplace accidents in the storage and warehousing industries. Over 1,700 of these accidents are major injuries including fractures and amputation
20 injuries. The number of accidents that occur is a clear indication that employers need to be taking more precautions to ensure the safety of their workers.

1. Which types of injuries are mentioned?

2. What are the reasons for the workplace accidents?

3. How could the risks of workplace accidents be reduced?

2.2.5 MEDIATION

Your manager needs the basic statements of the article for an internal training session. Unfortunately, he does not speak and understand English at all. He wants you to make a mediation of lines 8 to 17.

> **SKILLS**
> **Mediation**
> To mediate a text means to sum up the main ideas and essential information the reader is looking for. Adapt your mediation to the reader's needs and feel free to leave out less important information. You do not have to translate the text.

Warehouse Safety

2.2.6 INTERNET RESEARCH

Search the Internet for the keywords "forklift fatalities" to find more cases where forklifts were involved in serious accidents. Present your case to the class and explain what happened. Afterwards, start a discussion how to prevent such cases.

WORD BANK

ankle	Fußgelenk, Fußknöchel
to become familiar with sth.	mit etwas vertraut werden
bruise	Prellung, Bluterguss
compensation	Schmerzensgeld, Schadensersatz
concrete floor	Betonboden
to crush	quetschen, zerdrücken
fatality	Unglück, Todesfall
fireproof	feuerfest, feuerbeständig
hazard	Gefahr, Risiko
injury	Verwundung, Verletzung
to kneel down	sich hinknien, niederknien
measure	Maßnahme
to occur	auftreten
precautions	Vorsichtsmaßnahmen
to prohibit	verbieten
severe	ernst, schlimm, schwer
slips and trips	Rutschgefahr
theft	Diebstahl
threat	Drohung, Gefährdung

HOW TO USE

Simple Past		
Anwendung:		
wenn abgeschlossene Ereignisse oder Handlungen, die in der Vergangenheit stattgefunden haben, ausgedrückt werden sollen, Signalwörter: yesterday, last month, two days ago, in 2022, then, at that time etc.		We receiv**ed** the delivery **last week**. He clean**ed** the warehouse **yesterday**.
Bildung: Simple Past = Verb + "**ed**" oder 2. Form des Verbs		
Positive Aussage	**Verneinung**	**Frage – Kurzantwort**
I/you check**ed** it	I/you **didn't** check it	**Did** I/you check it? – Yes, you/I **did**. / No, you/I **didn't**.
he/she/it check**ed** it	he/she/it **didn't** check it	**Did** he/she/it check it? – Yes, he/she/it **did**. / No, he/she/it **didn't** it.
we/you/they check**ed** it	we/you/they **didn't** check it	**Did** we/you/they check it? – Yes, we/you/they **did**. / No, we/you/they **didn't** it.

Warehouse Safety

Simple Past		
Achtung: – endet der Infinitiv auf "e", entfällt dieses, z.B. phone – phon**ed**; – nach kurzem Vokal wird der Konsonant am Ende des Verbs verdoppelt, z.B. stop – stop-ped, plan – planned; – endet der Infinitiv auf "y", verwandelt sich dieses in ein "i", z.B. carry – carried		
Ausnahme: Verb "to be"		
Positive Aussage	**Verneinung**	**Frage – Kurzantwort**
I **was**	I **wasn't**	**Was** I? – Yes, you **were**. / No, you **weren't**.
you **were**	you **weren't**	**Were** you? – Yes, I **was**. / No, I **wasn't**.
he/she/it **was**	he/she/it **wasn't**	**Was** he/she/it? – Yes, he/she/it **was**. / No, he/she/it **wasn't**.
we/you/they **were**	we/you/they **weren't**	**Were** we/you/they? – Yes, we/you/they **were**. / No, we/you/they **weren't**.

2.2.7 EXERCISE

Put the verbs into the Simple Past.

Tom (1) _____ (found) the company in 1999 and

(2) _____ (start) with six employees. They

(3) _____ (work) very hard at the beginning and

(4) _____ (be) happy that the company

(5) _____ (sell) their innovative products on the market.

The number of customers (6) _____ (rise) constantly which

(7) _____ (lead) to a lack of capacity. Therefore, Tom

(8) _____ (decide) to enlarge the company. In 2001, workers

(9) _____ (finish) building the warehouse with approximately 2,000 square metres.

Soon, they (10) _____ (buy) warehouse equipment such as

forklift trucks, pallet trucks and a shelving system. They even (11) _____

Warehouse Safety

2

(purchase) two lorries which (12) _____ (allow) them to deliver the goods directly to their customers and business partners. Looking back, Tom's decision to invest in a warehouse (13) _____ (be) the right one and no one doubts that the warehouse has become one of the most efficient and well-structured departments.

Last year, the company (14) _____ (celebrate) ten years of warehousing.

2.2.8 EXERCISE

Complete the sentences with one of these verbs. Put the verb into the correct form, positive or negative.

| be | cost | enjoy | go | have | show | spend | stop | travel | visit |

1. I was very tired, so I (1) _____ to bed early.

2. The book wasn't very expensive. It (2) _____ very much.

3. I (3) _____ by train with friends through Europe and we (4) _____ a lot of interesting places.

4. Did you (5) _____ her the photos of your trip to China last year?

5. It was very hard work unloading the container. The boxes (6) _____ very heavy and bulky.

6. The PC game wasn't very exciting. I (7) _____ it very much.

7. Paul (8) _____ a lot of money on clothes and PC equipment last month. Therefore, he (9) _____ making payments on his credit card.

8. I was in a hurry, so I (10) _____ time to e-mail you.

2

Warehouse Safety

2.3 Health and Safety Hazards

2.3.1 LISTENING

Listen to the report about safety in the warehouse. Which of the following hazards are mentioned? Underline the correct ones.

> a lack of concentration | a nasty boss | broken glass | bad weather | drunk worker | lack of communication | long working hours | loud music | open fire | playing children | private problems | regular training | too heavy objects | wires or cables on the floor

Safety in the Warehouse

1 Working in a warehouse can be dangerous, but it does not have to be. Besides workplace hazards, many injuries come from worker safety issues like **manual handling** injuries. Manual handling injuries are quite **common,** especially among **novice** warehouse workers. These injuries can be caused by lifting heavy objects, long hours of carrying heavy loads, pulling
5 items, pushing cargo items, and even holding such items. Sometimes a bad movement or just long hours at work can cause severe injuries. Before hiring employees, training should be given to new employees on lifting techniques, stretches and good **posture**. This training should be repeated every few months for all employees.

Other risks may come from hazards in the warehouse. These hazards include items lying
10 around the platforms and workspace, not paying attention, lack of communication between employees and anything that seems out of place. There are ways to **avoid** such hazards. Some of these safety regulations may include daily **inspections** of the warehouse looking for possible hazards, speaking with the workers about potential safety hazards, or creating a team of employees to go over past cases of worker injuries and warehouse hazards in order to **pinpoint**
15 those hazards and injuries that are most common in your warehouse, and to work on solutions.

Sometimes there are many accidents in the workplace because of the layout design of the warehouse. Warehouses should have **ample** space to move about. Since workers are carrying heavy loads, the space should be open to avoid anyone **bumping** into anything. To decrease manual handling injuries the weight of objects carried should not **exceed** the weight that a
20 worker can carry, push, pull, etc. Items should also be easy to carry. If items are hard to hold onto, **oddly** shaped or easily droppable there should be other options provided to carry these items in order to avoid injuries.

In order to eliminate the hazards in a warehouse and to increase warehouse safety, the **entire staff** needs to work as a team. If there are items lying around, like broken glass, wires or cables,
25 these hazards should be reported to supervisors. Safety should always be every company's number one concern. If the workers are injured, no business will take place. But if the workers stay safe and obey workers' safety regulations in the warehouse, then the company can make a profit.

Warehouse Safety

2.3.2 READING

Read the text and put these paragraph summaries in the correct order.

- [ ] Teamwork is the key to successful occupational safety in a warehouse.
- [ ] In order to prevent manual handling injuries, special training should be given to the staff.
- [ ] The structure of the warehouse itself as well as the shape, weight and size of the goods determine the risks.
- [ ] Laws, regulations and internal guidelines include a broad range of measures to avoid accidents and injuries.

2.3.3 VOCABULARY WORK

Find ten nouns from the text "Safety in the Warehouse" in the word puzzle.

H	P	V	P	R	O	F	I	T	T	Y	W	V
Y	Q	Y	A	C	C	I	D	E	N	T	S	G
I	K	M	H	O	O	Y	I	A	J	Y	U	G
O	H	Z	X	C	L	N	C	N	T	U	J	I
G	D	Y	O	L	J	S	E	E	A	P	W	K
V	K	P	G	U	W	O	S	E	S	C	O	H
H	H	H	R	E	L	U	M	B	S	G	Z	T
F	O	I	I	U	O	K	P	L	Q	J	G	F
Q	E	G	F	H	G	N	I	N	I	A	R	T
S	H	I	E	E	M	P	L	O	Y	E	E	S
T	C	R	Y	N	A	P	M	O	C	X	Q	S
A	A	E	C	A	P	S	K	R	O	W	G	O
W	N	H	E	T	B	U	S	I	N	E	S	S

WORD BANK

ample	geräumig, ausgiebig
to avoid	verhindern
to bump into sth./so.	mit etwas/jemandem zusammenstoßen
common	alltäglich, häufig, bekannt
entire	ganz, komplett
to exceed	übertreffen
inspection	Prüfung, Kontrolle
manual handling	manuelle Handhabung
novice	Anfänger, Neuling
odd	seltsam
to pinpoint	genau bestimmen, festlegen
posture	Haltung, Körperhaltung

Warehouse Safety

HOW TO USE

Pronouns		
Anwendung:		
Pronomen sind sogenannte Fürwörter. Sie ersetzen ein Substantiv und vermeiden dadurch eine Wiederholung des gleichen Wortes in einem Satz.		The lorry was late, **it** had been delayed.
Arten von Pronomen:		
1. **hinweisende** Fürwörter (Demonstrativpronomen)		this, that, these, those Example: **These** letters were inquiries, **those** are offers.
2. Fürwörter, die **am Anfang von Nebensätzen** stehen (Relativpronomen)		who, whose, which, that, whoever Example: It was the first phone call **that** I received this morning.
3. **fragende** Fürwörter (Interrogativpronomen)		who, what, where Example: **Who** did you send for?
4. **persönliche** Fürwörter (Personalpronomen), drei Arten:		
Subjektpronomen	Objektpronomen	Possessivpronomen
Example: **I** like to drive a forklift.	Example: My girlfriend loves **me** but not **him**.	Example: This safety helmet is **mine**.
I	me	mine
you	you	yours
he/she/it	him/her/it	his/her/its
we	us	ours
you	you	yours
they	them	theirs

2.3.4 EXERCISE

Fill the gaps with the correct pronoun.

1. My name is Paul. (1) _____ am German. My mother's name is Ellen. (2) _____ is from Ireland. Karl is my dad. (3) _____ is an office clerk.

2. Our manager would like my colleague or (4) _____ to ring up the customer. My best friends live far away. (5) _____ sometimes visit me.

3. Susan and Carol started their apprenticeship last month. Paul left the warehouse earlier with (6) _____ .

Warehouse Safety

4. Did you or (7) _____ speak with the purchasing department?
5. Carol wants to get a driver's licence next year. The workbook is for (8) _____ .
6. Here is another invoice. I don't know what to do with (9) _____ .
7. My friends and I love ice cream. These ice lollies are for (10) _____ .

2.3.5 EXERCISE

Fill the gaps with either "who" or "which".

1. The driver came with another colleague (1) _____ waited inside the lorry.
2. My colleague (2) _____ worked at the goods receipt had an accident.
3. Give me the delivery note (3) _____ is in the office, please.
4. A warehouse operator is a person (4) _____ works in a store room.
5. Did you take the forklift truck (5) _____ was outside the warehouse?
6. Thank you very much for your leaflet, (6) _____ was very interesting.
7. I do not know the name of the colleague (7) _____ told me to unload the goods.

2.4 Safety Signs and Safety Clothing

2.4.1 MATCHING

Match the safety signs with the English expressions.

Prohibition signs	Fire safety signs	Emergency signs	Hazard warning signs	Mandatory signs
The safe way. Where to go in an emergency.	Location where you can find fire equipment.	You must do. Carry out the action given by the sign.	Caution. Risk of danger. Hazard ahead.	Stop. Do not. You must not.

Warehouse Safety

2.4.2 MATCHING

Match the expressions to the corresponding symbols.

> forklifts in operation | emergency meeting point | fire extinguisher | fire hose | first aid station | floating load | ear protection must be worn | no admittance | no storage or stacking | wear safety gloves

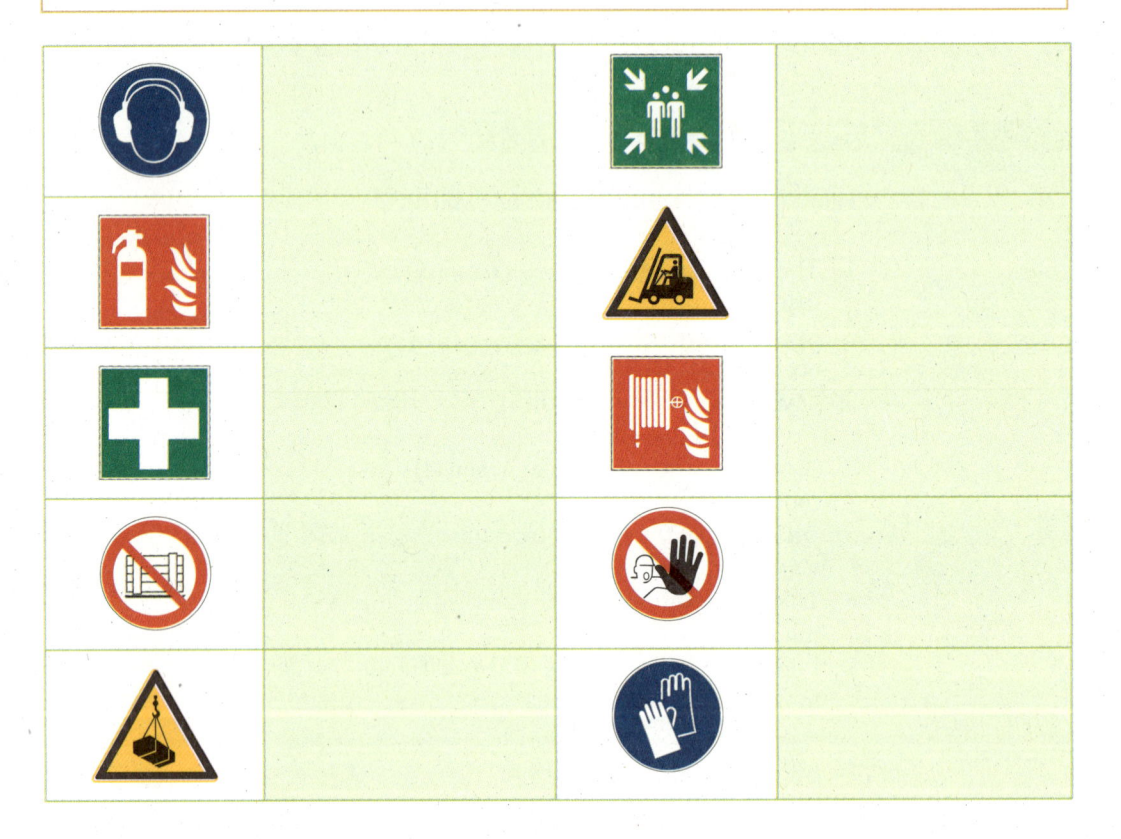

Symbol	Expression	Symbol	Expression
ear protection (blue circle, headphones)		emergency meeting point (green)	
fire extinguisher (red)		forklifts in operation (yellow triangle)	
first aid (green cross)		fire hose (red)	
no storage or stacking (red crossed circle)		no admittance (red crossed circle with hand)	
floating load (yellow triangle)		wear safety gloves (blue circle)	

2.4.3 WRITING

Describe the five types of safety signs with the words and phrases in the box.

> Colours: red and black on white | black on yellow | white on red | white on green | white on blue
> Shape: a circle | a triangle | a square | circular band with diagonal cross bar
> Meaning: prohibition | danger | alarm | warning | emergency escape | first aid | no danger | fire-fighting equipment | mandatory
> Instructions: specific behaviour or action | be careful | take precautions | dangerous behaviour | stop | identification and location | doors | exits

Warehouse Safety

2.4.4 MATCHING

Match the elements of personal protective equipment with the pictures.

> ear protection | goggles | safety boots with anti-slip sole | safety helmet | safety vest | skin protection | weather protective clothing | work gloves | work trousers

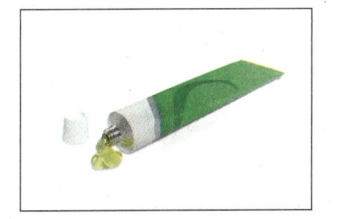

Warehouse Safety

2.5 Business Correspondence – E-Mails and Business Letters

2.5.1 BRAINSTORMING

Brainstorm with your neighbour how a buyer can find information about goods and suppliers. Make a list of information sources and present your findings to the class.

2.5.2 ANALYSING

Galaton is a supplier of safety equipment. Have a look at the company's website and answer the questions.

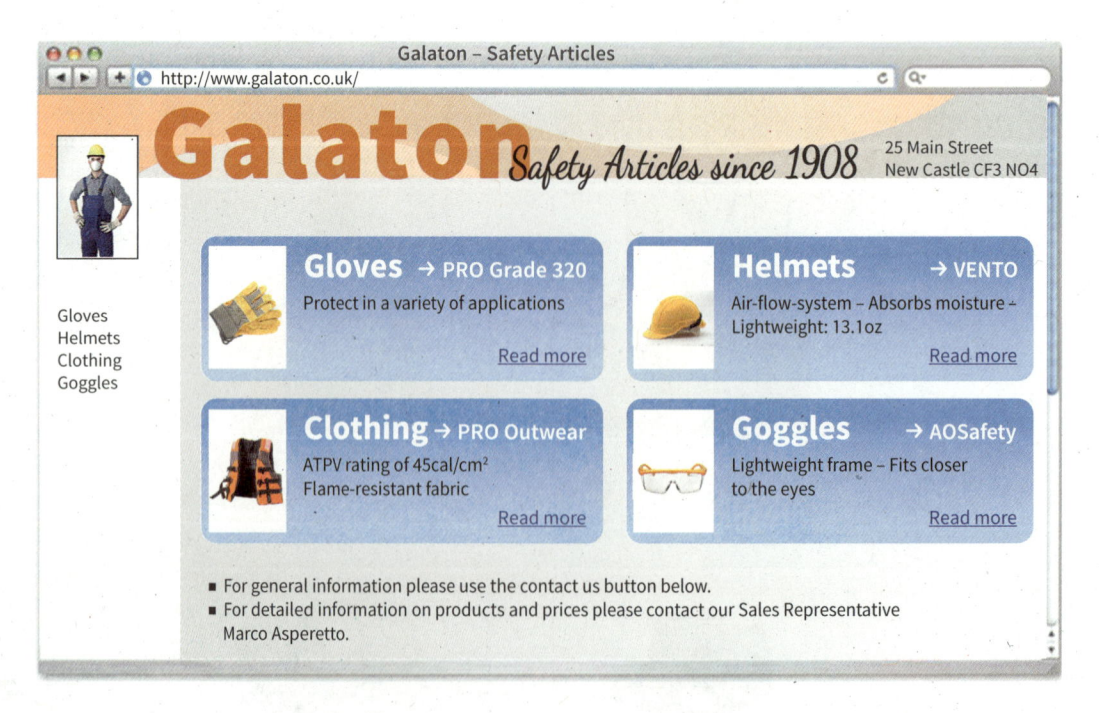

Galaton – Safety Articles
http://www.galaton.co.uk/

Galaton Safety Articles since 1908
25 Main Street
New Castle CF3 NO4

Gloves
Helmets
Clothing
Goggles

Gloves → PRO Grade 320
Protect in a variety of applications
Read more

Helmets → VENTO
Air-flow-system – Absorbs moisture – Lightweight: 13.1oz
Read more

Clothing → PRO Outwear
ATPV rating of 45cal/cm²
Flame-resistant fabric
Read more

Goggles → AOSafety
Lightweight frame – Fits closer to the eyes
Read more

- For general information please use the contact us button below.
- For detailed information on products and prices please contact our Sales Representative Marco Asperetto.

Warehouse Safety

1. Where is the company located?

2. Which products do they offer?

3. How can you contact Galaton for general information?

4. Who do you have to contact for more details?

2.5.3 MATCHING

Ronald Hensten of *Hensten Electrics* writes an e-mail to the sales representative of *Galaton*.

a. Match the numbered parts of the e-mail to the typical elements of an e-mail message.
b. Copy the list of elements of an e-mail message into your exercise book. Use a dictionary to translate them into German.

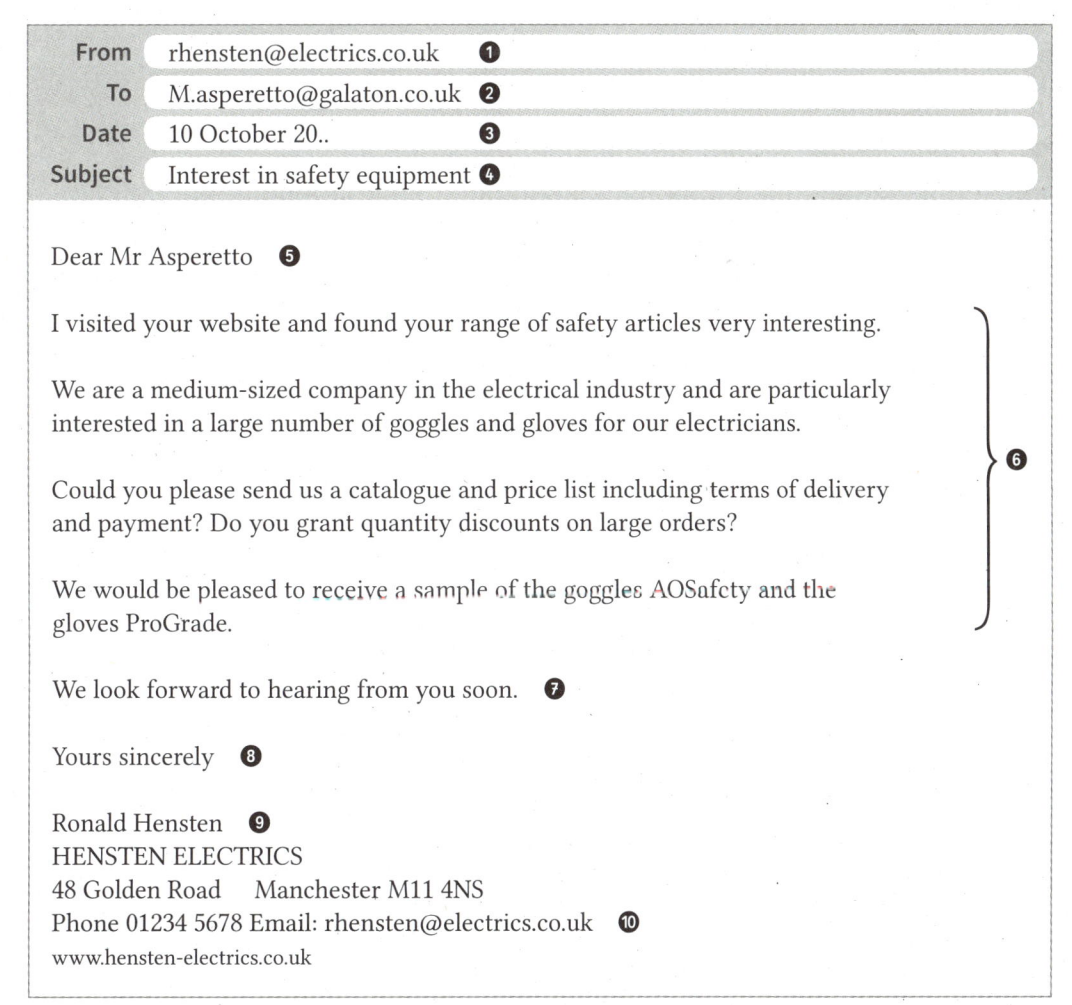

From	rhensten@electrics.co.uk ❶
To	M.asperetto@galaton.co.uk ❷
Date	10 October 20.. ❸
Subject	Interest in safety equipment ❹

Dear Mr Asperetto ❺

I visited your website and found your range of safety articles very interesting.

We are a medium-sized company in the electrical industry and are particularly interested in a large number of goggles and gloves for our electricians.

Could you please send us a catalogue and price list including terms of delivery and payment? Do you grant quantity discounts on large orders?

We would be pleased to receive a sample of the goggles AOSafety and the gloves ProGrade. ❻

We look forward to hearing from you soon. ❼

Yours sincerely ❽

Ronald Hensten ❾
HENSTEN ELECTRICS
48 Golden Road   Manchester M11 4NS
Phone 01234 5678 Email: rhensten@electrics.co.uk ❿
www.hensten-electrics.co.uk

☐ recipient's e-mail address – E-Mail-Adresse des Empfängers
☐ Bcc – blind carbon copy – Blindkopie
☐ salutation – Anrede
☐ sender's e-mail address – E-Mail-Adresse des Absenders
☐ footer (company name, address etc.) – Fußzeilen
☐ subject – Betreff
☐ date – Datum

☐ complimentary close – Grußformel
☐ sender's full name – Vollständiger Name des Absenders
☐ sender's position – Position des Absenders
☐ Cc – carbon copy – Kopie
☐ message – Nachricht
☐ goodwill phrase – Abschlusssatz (Wohlwollen erzeugen)
☐ attachment – Anhang

c. There are four items left in the list above. Discuss when and where they are used in an e-mail.

Warehouse Safety

2.5.4 MATCHING

Mr Hensten is in urgent need of safety gloves and goggles. As he has technical problems with his e-mail system, he decides to send a business letter to Mr Asperetto by snail mail. Complete the list below by matching the English parts of the business letter to their German translations.

Hensten Electrics

48 Golden Road   Manchester M11 4NS
Phone 01234 5678
Email: hensten@electrics.co.uk   **1. letterhead**

Our ref.: P/rh   **2. reference line**

15 October 20..   **3. date**

Mr Marco Asperetto
GALATON
25 High Street   **4. recipient's address**
Newcastle
NE3 NO4

Dear Mr Asperetto   **5. salutation**

Safety articles   **6. subject line**

I visited your website and found your range of safety articles very interesting.

We are a medium-sized company in the electric industry and are particularly interested in a large number of goggles and gloves for our electricians.

Could you please send us a catalogue and price list including terms of delivery and payment. Do you grant quantity discounts on large orders?   **7. body of the letter**

We would be pleased to receive a sample of the goggles AOSafety and of the gloves ProGrade.

We look forward to your early reply.

Yours sincerely   **8. complimentary close**

Ronald Hensten   **9. signature block**
Ronald Hensten
Manager

Empfängeradresse   Anrede

Unterschrift   Datum

Bezugszeichenzeile   Grußformel

Betreff   Brieftext

Briefkopf

2.5.5 ANALYSING

Now look at the parts of the e-mail on page 47 and find out the differences between the structure of an e-mail and the layout of a business letter. Discuss with your classmates.

	letter	e-mail		letter	e-mail
Letterhead	✓	–			

SKILLS — Useful tips for an appropriate style in business correspondence
- Express your ideas politely. Use words like "thank you", "please" and "would" or "could".
- Choose one-word constructions instead of phrasal verbs (to give back = to return, to fill in = to complete).
- Do not use capital letters – capitalising sounds like shouting at someone.
- Do not use abbreviations or contractions, write everything out in full, e. g. not "it's" but "it is".
- Do not use emoticons or text message abbreviations.

Note
In e-mails the word 'attachment/to attach' is used, whereas in business letters the word 'enclosure/to enclose' is used.

Warehouse Safety

2.5.6 MATCHING

Match the sentences 1 to 10 with the formal sentences a. to j.

1. I saw your goods on your website
2. Send me a pricelist with terms of payment.
3. I need the information now.
4. When can you deliver?
5. Can I get a discount?
6. We await your reply immediately.
7. The stuff was damaged.
8. The guy at your stand gave me a catalogue.
9. This is poor quality.
10. I'll order more articles if they are good.

a. Could you please send us your pricelist including terms of payment.
b. Please let me have your earliest delivery date.
c. If the articles sell well, we will place a substantial order.
d. Do you grant any discounts?
e. I have visited your website and found your products interesting.
f. We look forward to your early reply.
g. I visited your stand at the trade fair, where I obtained a catalogue of your products.
h. We would be grateful to receive the information as soon as possible.
i. Unfortunately, the products arrived in bad condition.
j. We regret to inform you that the quality of the product does not meet our requirements.

2.5.7 READING

You are Sam Manson. You work for Petersen & Co. Your boss, Christel Poly, left the following note on your desk.

Read through the note below and answer the following questions.

1. What has Ms Poly received?

2. Which article does Ms Poly want to order?

3. When does the company need the helmets?

4. What further information is needed?

2.5.8 WRITING

Use the structuring on page 47 and write the e-mail to Ms Mile.

Petersen & Co
10 – 14 Stephens Street | Manchester

NOTE

Date: 18. September 20..
From: Christel Poly
To: Sam Manson

Hi Sam

Can you please write an e-mail to Brown & Safe (Ms Gina Mile –gina-mile@bs.co.uk). We have received their catalogue for safety articles. The articles look good.

We would like to order helmets (yellow) for our staff and need them by the end of the month.

We need further information about the earliest delivery date and if they grant quantity discounts.

Christel

From:
To:
Date:
Subject:

Warehouse Safety

WORD BANK		
	delivery date	Liefertermin
	discount	Rabatt, Ermäßigung
	to grant	gewähren, einräumen
	grateful	dankbar
	range of	Auswahl/Angebot an
	to rephrase	umformulieren
	requirement	Anforderung
	substantial	umfangreich, beträchtlich
	terms of delivery	Lieferbedingungen
	terms of payment	Zahlungsbedingungen

2.5.9 CROSSWORD PUZZLE

Complete the crossword puzzle.

DOWN
1. Lager
2. Unfall
3. Gefahr
4. Palette
5. Sicherheit
9. Regal
10. Gabelstapler

ACROSS
6. Verletzung
7. beladen
8. beschädigen
11. transportieren
12. anheben

3 Receiving and Storing Goods

DISCUSSION

Look at the picture and describe what you see.

BRAINSTORMING

What do you or your colleagues do when your company receives a delivery? Exchange your experience with your neighbour and make a mind map from your results together. Put your mind map on a poster and prepare a short presentation. You may use the vocabulary from the box below. Decide who is going to present which part.

| unload lorry | check/sign | delivery note | count boxes | check for damage | compare delivery with order | put goods on pallets |

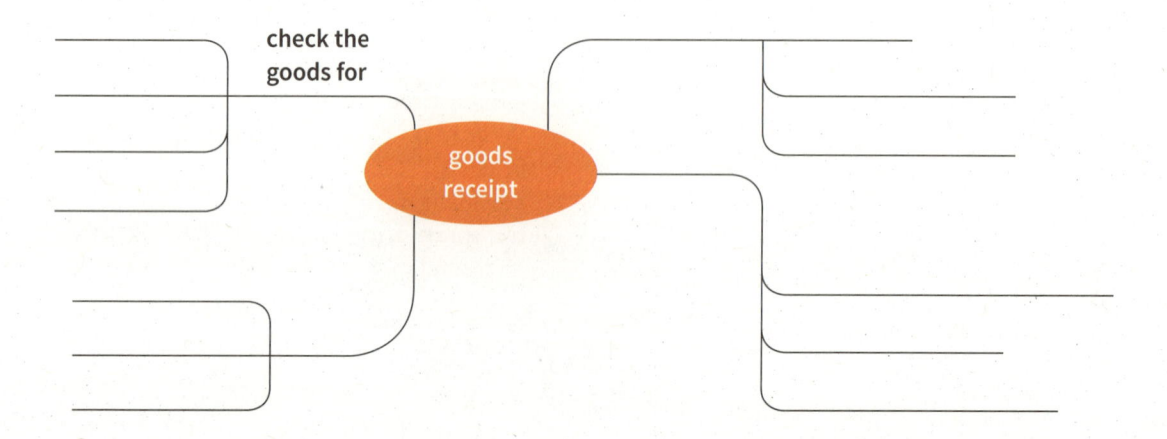

check the goods for

goods receipt

Receiving and Storing Goods

3

PRESENTATION

Present your mind map to the class. Try to speak in complete sentences and keep eye contact with the class and the teacher.

SKILLS

Tips for delivering professional presentations
1. Prepare yourself as best as you can (do research on the topic).
2. Watch your body language/non-verbal communication (facial expression, gestures, etc.).
3. Do not talk fast – pause for emphasis.
4. Keep it short and simple.
5. Do not read directly from your notes/slides – make eye contact.
6. Use visual aids such as photos and videos.
7. Make sure the extracted information corresponds with common quotation rules.
8. Follow the 10-20-30 rule (use 10 or fewer slides, keep it under 20 minutes and make your font size at least 30 point).

3.1 Receiving Goods

3.1.1 ANALYSING

a. There are different activities in the goods receiving department. Put them into the correct order. The order may vary from company to company and depend on the size and the type of industry.
b. Add the German translations.

a.
- [ ] check reusable packages
- [ ] sign delivery note
- [ ] count amount of packages
- [ ] inform purchasing department about noticed transport damage
- [ ] unload goods
- [ ] delivery of goods
- [ ] check condition of packages
- [ ] incoming goods inspection
- [ ] document noticed transport damage
- [ ] exchange reusable packages
- [ ] check address

b.

3 Receiving and Storing Goods

3.1.2 WRITING

Look at the chart again and write a short text about what warehouse operators have to do when they receive a consignment. Use the Simple Present (see „How to use – Simple Present", p. 13) and read your text to the class afterwards.

3.1.3 LISTENING FOR GIST

Listen carefully to the report on how goods have to be checked appropriately. Write down which four categories are checked by the warehouse staff.

3.1.4 LISTENING FOR DETAIL

Listen again and answer the following questions.

1. How do you check the identity of the goods?

2. How can you find out the quantity of goods?

3. What do you compare if you want to check the quality?

4. What does the term "goods delivered in apparently good condition" mean?

5. Name four documents the quality control department or the warehouse staff need for the check.

6. What do you enter into the stock list?

SKILLS

Listening for gist
Listening for gist means that it is not necessary to understand everything. You should merely try to get the core message. Do not get frustrated or demotivated if you are not able to identify all the words.

Receiving and Storing Goods

WORD BANK

apparently	anscheinend, augenscheinlich
to check	prüfen
condition	Zustand
delivery note	Lieferschein
to document	beurkunden, dokumentieren
to exchange sth.	etwas austauschen
offer	Angebot
order	Auftrag
purchasing department	Einkaufsabteilung
reusable	wieder verwendbar, Mehrweg …
to sign a receipt	eine Quittung unterschreiben
stock list	Lagerliste
to unload sth.	etwas abladen

3.1.5 READING

Read the text you have just listened to. With your neighbour, decide if the statements below the text are true (T) or false (F). If they are false, correct them.

Goods Receipt

1 As the warehouse is the *interface* between several departments it is very important to have good warehouse management with well-organised processes and procedures. The requirements of modern logistics are demanding and complex. Every day a lot of *consignments* arrive in various companies. Before the goods can be stored correctly the *delivery* has to be checked
5 by the goods receiving department. This part of the procedure is called "Goods Receipt". The warehouse operators inspect the incoming goods. The goods are registered here and locations are found before the articles are put *into stock*. In small companies there is often no goods receiving department and all the work is done by the normal warehouse staff, but in larger firms a separate department is recommended.

10 After the goods are unloaded the buyer has to check the delivery. For checking the identity you have to compare the delivery note with the contents of the packages. By counting the articles or packages you can find out if the amount is correct or not. Before the buyer opens the packages he inspects the condition of the shipment and checks that there is no visible damage. If everything looks all right, he signs a copy of the delivery note with the expression "goods
15 delivered in apparently good condition". He has to do that while the carrier is still present. Later, the buyer checks the quality of the goods, which is far more difficult. He has to check if the quality *corresponds to* what was ordered. He compares the *order* and the *offer* with the *packing list* and the *delivery note*, and other *forwarding documents* such as the *waybill* and the *air waybill*.

20 It is also very important to compare the offer with the *invoice* because the prices in the invoice must be identical to the prices in the offer. If everything is acceptable you enter the goods into the *stock list*. For this you enter the article number and the quantity that has arrived. As mentioned above, the buyer has to complain directly to the *carrier* in the case of any visible damage. Damaged goods or goods which have not been ordered have to be kept until the
25 supplier gives instructions what to do with them. The supplier has to be informed about any hidden damage or other mistakes directly after detection, without delay. In many companies several departments, for example purchasing, *accounting* or production, are informed about the arrived goods by a *goods receipt slip*. This can be a paper form or a data set.

Receiving and Storing Goods

TRUE (=T) OR FALSE (=F)?

1. Every company must have a "Goods Receiving Department".

2. You have to check the condition of the packages the day after the receipt of goods at the latest.

3. You have to keep faulty items in your company and wait for the supplier's directive.

4. Damage which isn't visible at first sight can be complained about within certain time limits.

5. A ten percent price difference between the offer and the invoice has to be accepted.

3.1.6 VOCABULARY WORK

Fill in the gaps with a word from the box.

complain | consignment | damage | delivery note | offer | in stock | order

1. The supplier will send us the (1) _____ tomorrow. We will check it and decide if we order a large amount.

2. The ordered goods from our supplier will probably arrive next week. UPS will deliver the (2) _____ to our company.

3. I always compare the (3) _____ with the order.

4. I don't know if we have enough articles (4) _____.

5. There are some packages with obvious (5) _____. We will complain about that immediately.

6. If the offer is very good we will place a larger (6) _____.

7. If there is damage we will have to (7) _____.

Receiving and Storing Goods

3.1.7 MEDIATION

Your manager has asked you to do a short training course for a new trainee about the duties of the buyer. He has asked you to mediate this text into German because the trainee doesn't speak any English (see „Skills – Mediation", p. 36).

Complaints

It is very important to complain about damage to the supplier and/or the carrier without delay. If both contract partners are business people, the buyer has to inspect the goods immediately and claim visible damages at once. Hidden damage must be complained about directly after detection, but not later than two years after delivery. Otherwise the buyer would lose his claim against
5   the supplier unless the supplier hasn't mentioned damage he knows about on purpose.

WORD BANK

accounting	Buchhaltung
air waybill	Luftfrachtbrief
carrier	Frachtführer
to complain about	reklamieren, sich über etwas beschweren
consignment/delivery/shipment	Lieferung
to correspond to	etwas entsprechen
forwarding documents	Warenbegleitpapiere
goods receipt slip	Wareneingangsschein
invoice	Rechnung
interface	Schnittstelle
in stock	vorrätig
packing list	Packliste
quality control	Qualitätskontrolle

HOW TO USE

Will-Future	
Anwendung:	
– um Vorhersagen oder Vermutungen auszudrücken	The prices **will** rise next year.
– für spontane Absichtserklärungen	Are you busy? I **will** help you.
– für Versprechen	I **will** load the lorry later.
Bildung: Will-Future = "will" + Verb	

Positive Aussage	Verneinung	Frage
I/you/he/she/it/we/you/they will read Kurzform: … 'll read	I/you/he/she/it/we/you/they will not read Kurzform: … won't read	Will I/you/he/she/it/we/you/they read?

3 Receiving and Storing Goods

3.1.8 EXERCISE

Fill in the correct form of the Will-Future.

1. The weather tomorrow (1) _____ (be) warm and sunny.

   There (2) _____ (not be) any rain.

2. My colleague said: "I (3) _____ (help) you with the lorry."

3. I think our company (4) _____ (not take) a new apprentice next year because our sales figures are not very good.

4. My brother said yesterday: "I (5) _____ (pick you up) after work."

5. Maybe the next consignment (6) _____ (arrive) next week.

6. I think my boss (7) _____ (not install) the new software before Monday.

7. We all hope that our economy (8) _____ (not get) worse again.

8. The new unemployment rate (9) _____ (be published) in November.

9. Our customer (10) _____ (be) very disappointed because you have forgotten to inform him about the delay.

10. I'm afraid my boss (11) _____ (not give) me a week off in July. We have a lot of work in July.

3.2 Registration of Goods Receipt

Goods Receipt Slip — Hensten Electrics

Number	85652/8	Date 20..-12-08
	20..-12-08	Time 14:35
		User Smith

Order number	125665	Supplier	Homag Ltd.
Delivery note number	7852/96		Liverpool
Invoice number	204588		

Article M_8_x_30   300 units

Raised countersunk M 8 x 30 according to DIN 966
Recessed head H,4,8 zinc-plated

Version   12/36
Charge number 233
Storage bin   B/135   36/658
Cost centre   002

Receiving and Storing Goods

3.2.1 MATCHING

Look at the form. Fill in the gaps below to match the English and German expressions with the numbers in the form.

1. Datum — _____
2. _____ — order number
3. _____ — _____
4. Artikelnummer — _____
5. Menge — _____
6. _____ — _____
7. Lagereinheit — _____

3.2.2 BRAINSTORMING

Work in pairs. Which information does a goods receipt slip need to contain? Which departments need a copy and why? Write your ideas on cards. Use different colours for the pieces of information and the departments.

Pin your cards with ideas from your pair work on the two posters when your teacher asks you to. If your idea is already there, give your card back to your teacher.

3.2.3 WRITING

Write a text about the goods receipt slip and its importance for the company. You can use the ideas from the posters. Read your text to the class afterwards.

Receiving and Storing Goods

HOW TO USE

If-Clauses, Type I	
Anwendung:	
Bedingungssätze (If-Clauses) bestehen aus einem if-Satz und einem Hauptsatz:	
Der **if-Satz** nennt eine realistische Bedingung: etwas, das eintreten kann, soll oder wird. **Bildung:** Simple Present	If we **work** on Saturday, … (Wenn wir am Samstag arbeiten, …)
Der **Hauptsatz** drückt aus, was passiert, wenn die Bedingung erfüllt ist. **Bildung:** will/can/must + Infinitiv	… we **will finish** this order next week. (… werden wir diesen Auftrag in der nächsten Woche beenden.)
Achtung: – if-Satz kann vor oder nach dem Hauptsatz stehen – niemals "will" im if-Satz verwenden	

3.2.4 EXERCISE

Circle the correct word(s) in each sentence.

1. If you *ring/will ring* this bell, the receptionist will come.
2. If you take your umbrella with you tomorrow, you *aren't/won't get* wet.
3. My mother will go to bed early if she *will feel/feels* tired.
4. The customer *will call/is called* later if the delivery doesn't arrive on time.
5. If it *rains/will rain* tomorrow, we won't load the lorry.
6. If you *don't hurry/won't hurry* up, we won't reach the plane.
7. If our teacher *is/will be* ill tomorrow, we won't have an English lesson.
8. I *will look/look* up the word if you lend me your dictionary.
9. If you *don't come/won't come* to work tomorrow, your company will send you a warning letter.
10. If you get a third warning letter, your boss *will fire/fires* you.

3.2.5 EXERCISE

Fill in the correct form of the verb. Use the If-Clause, Type I.

1. If it (1) _____ (rain) tomorrow, we

   (2) _____ (not be able) to load the lorry.

Receiving and Storing Goods

2. If we (3) _____ (not order) the new items next week, our customers (4) _____ (have to) wait.

3. All the apprentices (5) _____ (receive) a bonus if they (6) _____ (execute) the orders on time.

4. My teacher (7) _____ (give) me a good mark if I (8) _____ (be) active in his lessons in the coming weeks.

5. If you (9) _____ (not hurry) up, you (10) _____ (miss) the bus.

6. If the new colleague (11) _____ (not enter) the article into the stock list, it (12) _____ (be) difficult to know what we have in stock.

7. If the taxi (13) _____ (not come) soon, we (14) _____ (miss) our plane.

8. What (15) _____ you _____ (do) if your boss (16) _____ (not let) you take a day off?

9. I (17) _____ (give) you a lift if your car (18) _____ (be) still at the garage after work.

10. I (19) _____ (phone) our customers if the delivery (20) _____ (be) late.

3.2.6 INTERNET RESEARCH

There are three main ways to register the goods which have been received. Search the Internet and inform yourself about one of these ways. Prepare a short presentation in English.

1. Barcode or label (1-D-Codes and 2-D-Codes)
2. Serial Shipping Container Code (SSCC)
3. Radio Frequency Identification (RFID)

3 Receiving and Storing Goods

> **SKILLS**
> If you have to do an Internet search, the following tips might be useful for you:
> 1. Think about the search words carefully.
> 2. Do not only work with one source – cross-check each piece of information.
> 3. Wikipedia is always a good start because it gives you an overview about the topic and useful links at the end.
> 4. Use only original, reliable sources and not texts which are only based on them.

3.3 Storing Goods

3.3.1 MATCHING

Match the following articles and their need for protection and write them into the corresponding column.

dairy products | flower soil | fruit and vegetables | grain | paper | technical devices | textiles

Protection against	Examples
sunlight	
loss of taste	
humidity	
vermin	
heat/cold	
drying up	

3.3.2 READING

Read the following text about the correct storage of goods and answer the questions below the text.

Storing Goods under Appropriate Conditions

1   There are many aspects to **consider** if you want to store the delivered goods **appropriately**. It is not sufficient to keep the warehouse tidy and **well-arranged**. Different goods require different storage. Milk, cheese and butter, for example, must be **protected from** heat whereas tobacco products must be kept warm and dry. Wrong **treatment** or handling can cause serious damage
5   that is often expensive or even dangerous. Therefore a lot of rules have to be **followed** and warning signs are put up to **prevent** damage, accidents, fires etc.

Warehouse operators know the best conditions for their products and take measures against heat, cold and other conditions which are not **favourable** for the stored goods. As the employers are responsible for the safety of people and the goods in the warehouse they hand out

Receiving and Storing Goods

10 instructions their staff have to sign and follow. But there are also handling signs on many packages to show how to handle them properly.

The symbols for package handling instructions are internationally standardised in ISO R/780 (International Organization for Standardization) and in DIN 55 402 (DIN, German Institute for Standardization). The symbols must never be **omitted** as they are self-explaining and so over-
15 come language problems in international transport operations. Therefore, it is not difficult for new employees or apprentices to **gain** solid knowledge and experience about correct handling.

1. How does a warehouse have to be kept properly?

2. Which conditions that products have to be prevented from are mentioned in the text?

3. Why is it so important to know which conditions are best for each product?

4. Why do the employees have to follow rules and safety instructions?

WORD BANK	
appropriate	angemessen
by heart	auswendig
to consider	in Erwägung ziehen, betrachten
favourable	günstig
to gain	erlangen, aneignen
to follow rules/instructions	Regeln/Anweisungen befolgen
to omit	weglassen
to protect from	schützen vor
vermin	Schädlinge

3.3.3 MATCHING

Match the symbols and their meaning.

do not use forklift truck here | fragile, handle with care | keep away from heat | keep dry | protect from heat and radioactive sources | do not stack | top | use no hooks

65

3 Receiving and Storing Goods

3.4 Correct Storage

3.4.1 MATCHING

Work with your neighbour and read the little text below. Match the pictures and the corresponding words below. Talk with your neighbour about the types of storage you have in your company. Make a list with the articles you store in different ways and report to the class afterwards.

Storage Types

1 The appropriate storage of each item in stock is difficult and totally depends on the nature of the article, the type of the company, the location of the stock, the owner of the product and many further aspects. That's why you can distinguish the storage types in various ways. There are, for example, different sorts of racking systems like flat or high-rise storage as well as cen‑
5 tral or local and open or closed storage.

Receiving and Storing Goods

3.4.2 BRAINSTORMING

Many big companies have fully automatic warehouse equipment like conveyor belts, packing stations etc. that works non-stop. This only makes sense if it is used continuously and the process is standardised.

What are the advantages and the disadvantages of this modern technology for a company and for the employees? Brainstorm and collect your ideas on the (active) board.

3.4.3 WRITING

Write a short text about the advantages and disadvantages of fully automatic warehouse equipment. Use the phrases in the word bank below and evaluate the technology through the eyes of both the employer and the employees. Finish your text with a personal conclusion.

WORD BANK		
	as a result	schlussfolgernd
	first of all	zuerst, zuallererst
	furthermore	außerdem, darüber hinaus
	in addition	ergänzend, hinzu kommt
	in my opinion	meiner Meinung nach
	last but not least	nicht zuletzt
	on the one hand, on the other hand	auf der einen Seite, auf der anderen Seite
	therefore	somit, deshalb
	to sum it up	um es zusammenzufassen
	whereas	wobei, wohingegen
	while	während

3 Receiving and Storing Goods

3.5 Storage Systems

Storage Systems

1 There are also a lot of different systems for storing the products in a warehouse. But first of all you have to organise in which order you want to store the different articles and in which order you want to extract them for your orders. You have to number your corridors and aisles so that you will be able to find each item immediately. It is also important to store the goods in a way
5 that the employees always have the shortest route possible.

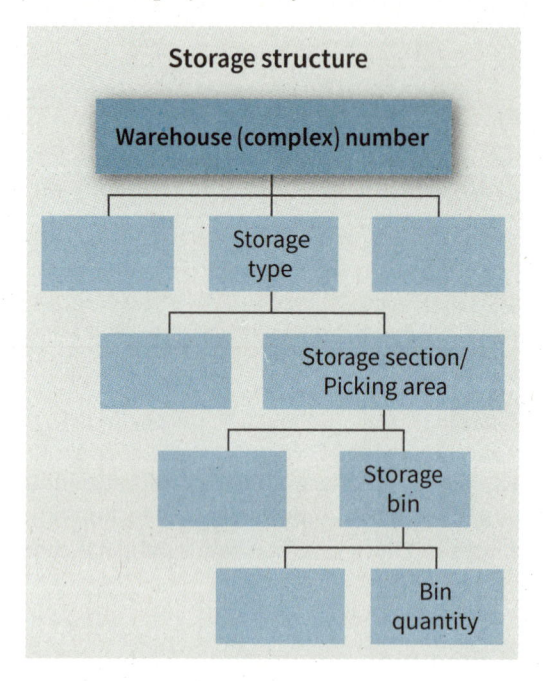

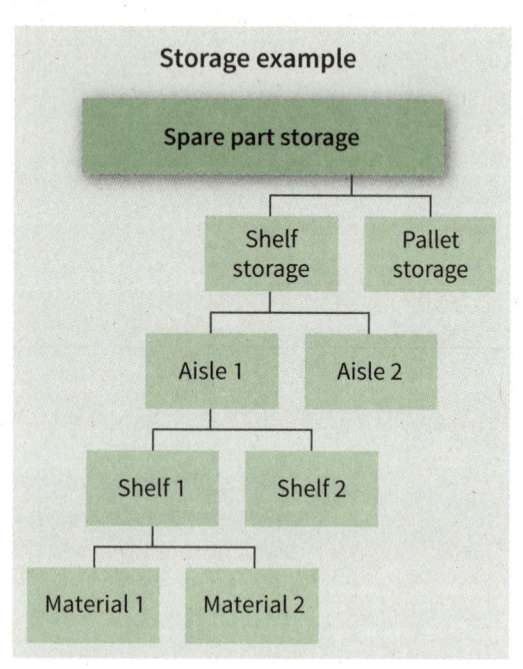

Storage structure
- Warehouse (complex) number
  - Storage type
    - Storage section/Picking area
      - Storage bin
        - Bin quantity

Storage example
- Spare part storage
  - Shelf storage
    - Aisle 1
      - Shelf 1
        - Material 1
      - Shelf 2
        - Material 2
    - Aisle 2
  - Pallet storage

3.5.1 PRESENTATION

Team up and take one topic from the following list. Tell your teacher which topic you have chosen. Inform yourselves about the topic and prepare a presentation about it.

1. GTIN-13 (former EAN)
2. ISBN-13-Code
3. Organisation of shelves
4. FIFO
5. LIFO
6. HIFO
7. Storage zones

3.5.2 ANALYSIS

Illustrate the storage structure of your warehouse. Interview colleagues and your manager about why this structure was established. If necessary, use an extra sheet.

3 Receiving and Storing Goods

3.6 Hazardous Goods

3.6.1 MATCHING

For the handling of dangerous or hazardous goods a worldwide standardised system (GHS) has been developed. It consists of nine pictograms. Look up the following words on the Internet or in your dictionary and write the correct expression under each symbol.

compressed gas | corrosive | dangerous to the environment | explosive | flammable | may cause cancer or genetic defects | oxidizing | toxic | warning

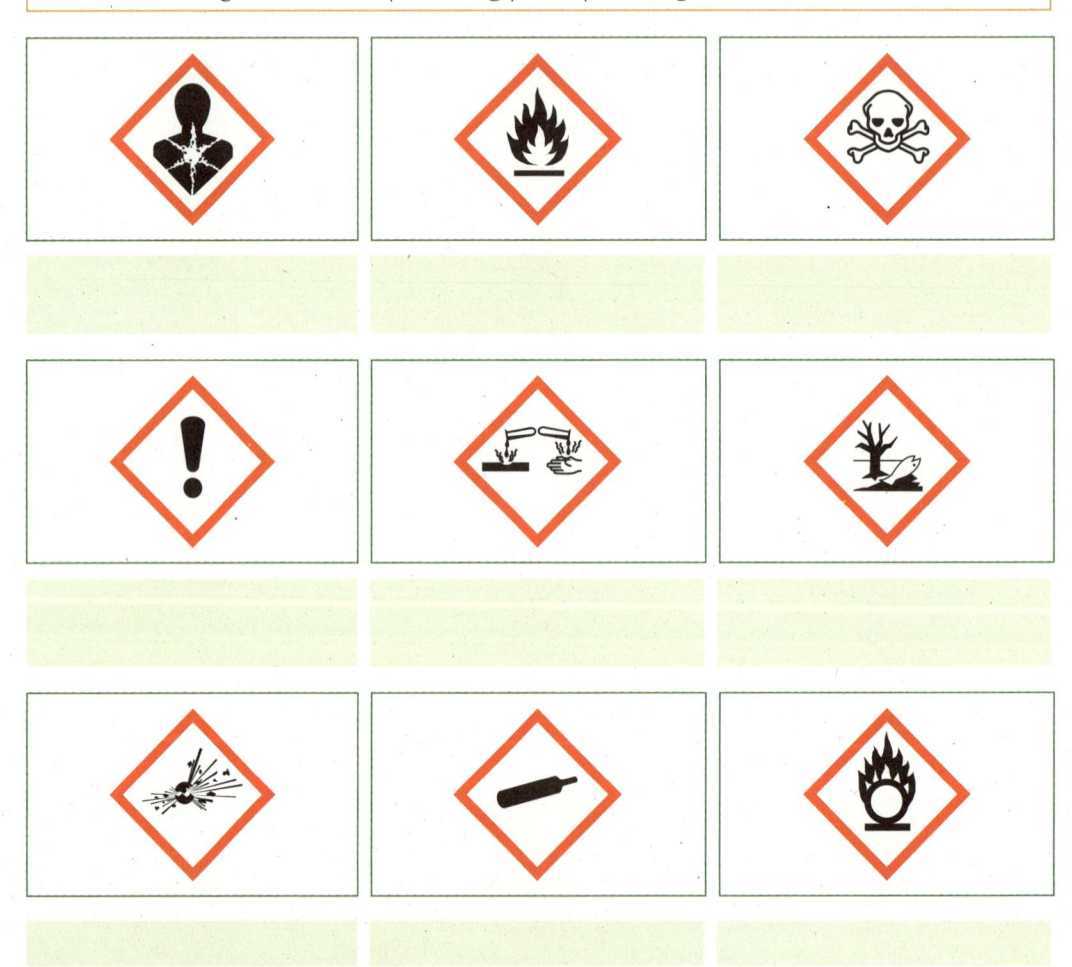

3.6.2 MEDIATION

Your boss has given you the following text in German and has asked you to translate it into English for the trainee from England. Use the vocabulary from the box below.

1 Das Arbeiten im Lager kann manchmal gefährlich sein. Deshalb muss jeder Arbeitgeber seinen Mitarbeitern auf einfache und verständliche Art erklären, wie sie mit gefährlichen Gütern arbeiten müssen. Außerdem müssen Warntafeln im Lager die Gefahrensymbole erklären. Ferner muss der Arbeitgeber erklären, wie die Mitarbeiter sich im Gefahrenfall verhalten sollen und
5 wie man erste Hilfe leisten kann. Abschließend muss er zeigen, wie man Abfälle richtig entsorgt.

to dispose of waste | to give first aid | in an easy and understandable way | in case of danger

3 Receiving and Storing Goods

3.7 Business Correspondence – Enquiries

3.7.1 READING

Read the following text about the definition of an enquiry and complete it with the words from the box.

brochure | discounts | nature | prospective | payment | presentation | price | request | terms

In a business context, an enquiry is a (1) _____ for information. Before ordering goods or services, the (2) _____ customer is likely to require details about the goods in question. An important piece of information for the buyer is the (3) _____ of the goods and the (4) _____ which the seller will be able to supply at. There are many questions to be clarified: Is the supplier in a position to grant (5) _____ e. g. on large orders? What are the (6) _____ of delivery? Which terms of (7) _____ are applied? Additionally, the buyer may ask for a catalogue or a (8) _____ and sometimes for samples of the goods. For specific goods, it might be necessary to arrange for a demonstration or (9) _____ on the buyer's premises.

3.7.2 MATCHING

Match the following words from the list to their German translation.

1. nature of the goods/service — a. Preis
2. price — b. Rabatt/Nachlass
3. discount — c. Beschaffenheit der Ware/Dienstleistung
4. terms of delivery — d. Lieferzeitpunkt
5. terms of payment — e. Zahlungsbedingungen
6. delivery time — f. Lieferbedingungen

3.7.3 EXERCISE

Complete the sentences in the following letter of enquiry.

Dear _____ or Madam

I _____ to your advertisement in the latest _____ of LOGIST.

We are a manufacturer of industrial tools and are _____ in the cardboard boxes you advertised.

_____ you please give me more _____ about your range of boxes, crates, shelves and pallets?

I would like to know your _____ of delivery and _____ as well as delivery times. Do you offer any _____?

I look forward to _____ soon.

Yours _____

Receiving and Storing Goods

3.7.4 READING

Read the enquiry for ratchet straps and answer the questions below.

FRESHLINE Ltd. 25 Benton Road * Newcastle NE27 6RU
Phone 0191 232 4233 • Fax: 0191 221 0138
E-Mail: freshline@food.co.uk
www.freshline-food.co.uk

Our ref.: RS-str
08 October 20..

GTF Cargo Control Ltd.
199 Broughton Road
Edinburgh
EH7 4LN

Dear Sir or Madam

I refer to your advertisement in the latest issue of Business Magazine which has drawn our attention to your products.

We are a large company specialising in food production for the catering industry. For the transport of our freshly produced food we are looking for reliable loading equipment. We are particularly interested in your new Heavy Duty Ratchet Straps.

Could you please send us general information including technical data on the above mentioned lashing equipment. We would be pleased to receive a brochure including prices and terms of delivery and payment. Please let us know if you grant quantity discounts on substantial orders.

We look forward to hearing from you soon.

Yours faithfully

Peter Straw

Peter Straw

---

1. Where did Mr Straw find out about GTF Cargo Control Ltd.?

2. What does he want them to send him?

3. Which elements of a business letter are missing?

3.7.5 EXERCISE

Read the following letter and fill in the correct prepositions from the box

of | about | to | to | from | by | together | at | for | in

Dear Mr Jones

We visited your stand ____at____ the Hanover Fair and found your range ____of____ products very interesting.

Our company is located ____in____ Manchester and produces spare parts for the automotive industry.

We are planning to purchase a number of safety goggles ____for____ our staff.

We need different sizes ____from____ small ____to____ extra large.

Could you please let us have further information ____about____ the suitable models ____together____ with a quotation.

A visit ____by____ your sales representative would be appreciated.

We look forward ____to____ hearing from you soon.

Yours sincerely

3.7.6 WRITING

You work for Atlas Products, a medium-sized company located in 13 Edward Court, London HA1 8NY. Your company is in urgent need of pallets for the warehouse. On Wesco's website you saw that they offer a new type of plastic pallets.
Write an enquiry to Wesco & Sons, 104 Stratford Avenue, Liverpool AB3 DE6:

- say how you learned about the company
- introduce your company
- ask for a catalogue and price list
- ask for terms of delivery and delivery time
- say that you will place a substantial order if prices are competitive

3 Receiving and Storing Goods

SKILLS

Structuring and wording of a letter of enquiry

1 Say where you found out about the company

We saw / I refer to	your advertisement	**for**	laser printers	**in**	*Tech Magazine* **of** 2 October. / the October issue **of** Tools & Co.
We have visited your website and					
We saw your products at the Machine Tools Exhibition in …					

2 Introduce your business

We are a	medium-sized/large well-established	company firm	producing specialising **in**	a wide range of … sophisticated …

3 Explain the reason for your enquiry

We are	planning to expand our storage area interested in expanding our business. interested in your products.

4 Say what you require

Could you please / Please	send us let us have enclose	information brochures **about** full details **of** a catalogue **of** a price list **for**	the services you offer. your latest products. your range of … your …

We	require would be grateful for	details of information on	your the	prices and discounts. terms of payment and delivery. delivery periods.

A visit by your representative A demonstration **on** our premises A presentation of your services	would be appreciated.

5 Close the letter

If your prices are competitive, we may be able to place large orders in the near future.
We hope to hear from you soon.

We	look forward are looking forward	to	hearing from you soon. an early reply.

6 Complimentary Close

Yours faithfully Yours sincerely

7 Mention enclosures

Enclosure(s): Price List   or   Encs.: 5 Leaflets   or   Enclosure(s)   or   Enc.

Receiving and Storing Goods

HOW TO USE

Countable and Uncountable Nouns	
Anwendung:	
Nomen können **zählbar** oder **unzählbar** sein.	
Zählbare Nomen (countable nouns) bezeichnen Dinge, die man zählen kann. – Sie haben eine Singular- und eine Pluralform. – Das begleitende Verb steht entsprechend entweder im Singular oder im Plural.	one lorry – two lorries one pallet – two pallets one office – four offices The helmet **is** yellow. The helmets **are** yellow.
Unzählbare Nomen (uncountable nouns) bezeichnen Dinge, die man nicht zählen kann. – Sie haben keine Pluralform. – Sie können nicht mit „a", „an" oder einem Zahlwort verwendet werden. – Das begleitende Verb steht immer im Singular. – Um Angaben über die Menge von unzählbaren Nomen zu machen, nennt man ein zählbares Nomen vorweg.	~~a~~ money ~~a~~ furniture ~~an~~ information ~~one~~ equipment The information about you **is** interesting. Our new safety equipment **is** very helpful. information – a piece of information data – two sets of data advice – a piece of advice
Achtung: Manche Nomen sind im Deutschen zählbar, nicht aber in ihrer englischen Entsprechung.	It's interesting **work**. – Es ist **eine** interessante **Arbeit**. I've got good **news** for you. – Ich habe **eine** gute **Nachricht** für Sie.

3.7.7 EXERCISE

Fill the blanks with the words in brackets using "a" or "an" where necessary.

ACD Production was planning to redecorate their offices, therefore the manager was looking for (1) _____ information about (2) _____ new office furniture. On the Internet he saw (3) _____ advertisement for chairs, desks and filing cabinets. He clicked on the call-back button. The next day, the company's representative gave him (4) _____ call back. He was of (5) _____ great help to him on how to plan the renovation of the offices.

Anne was searching for (6) _____ work. She went to the job agency where they gave her (7) _____ useful advice. Finally, they offered her (8) _____ job at the airport. She had enough (9) _____ experience in the travel business, so Anne got the job. Now she works at the check-in counter. Some people carry (10) _____ heavy luggage to the check-in point.

Receiving and Storing Goods

3.7.8 EXERCISE

Use the words from the box to make the nouns countable.

| a bag of | a bottle of | a cup of | a kilo of | a piece of | a slice of |

1. _____ coffee
2. _____ luggage
3. _____ paper
4. _____ information
5. _____ potatoes
6. _____ mineral water
7. _____ bread
8. _____ advice
9. _____ furniture
10. _____ cheese

3.7.9 EXERCISE

Translate into English.

1. Wir benötigen weitere Informationen über die Größe der Artikel.

2. Wir möchten 50 Schutzbrillen in Größe M bestellen.

3. Susan hat eine Tasse Kaffee mit Milch bestellt.

4. Allan hat einen Muffin bestellt.

5. Morgen bekommen wir neue Büromöbel und neue Computer.

6. Dann können wir die wichtigen Daten an unsere Kunden übermitteln.

Receiving and Storing Goods 3

WORD BANK		
	advice	Rat, Empfehlung
	competitive	wettbewerbsfähig
	delivery time	Lieferzeitpunkt, Lieferfrist
	enquiry	Anfrage
	filing cabinet	Aktenschrank
	located	ansässig
	luggage	Gepäck
	medium-sized	mittelständisch
	pallet	Palette
	to redecorate	renovieren

3.7.10 CROSSWORD PUZZLE

Complete the crossword puzzle.

ACROSS
9. the company you deliver to
10. to take action so that something does not happen
11. a big transport vehicle
12. to do something in order to make sure that everything is correct
13. another word for shipment
14. when things or people are very untidy and disorganised
15. a particular part of a place, city or country
16. British word for bill
17. Our company signed a three year ... with this supplier.
18. you store your goods under ... conditions
19. a printed piece of paper that shows that you have paid to travel or see a film
20. not in good condition

DOWN
1. you take these when you want to store your goods correctly
2. the company that delivers to you
3. to express dissatisfaction
4. it is not just urgent but it is ... urgent
5. if you can use something again, it is ...
6. I would like to ... my own business.
7. reduction in the usual price of something
8. the colleagues who keep our financial records work in the ...

4 Order Picking and Packing Goods

Order Picking

Order picking is one of a logistic warehouse's processes. Order picking means that the order picker extracts a small number of goods from a warehousing system. The order picker has to deal with a number of independent customer orders. Picking processes have become an important part of the supply chain process. Picking is seen as the most labour-intensive and costly activity for almost every warehouse. The cost of order picking is estimated
5 to be as much as 55 percent of the total warehouse operating expenses. There has been an increasing number of process improvements. They help companies to reduce costs and to meet the customer's needs.

DISCUSSION

Work together with your neighbour and answer the following questions.

a. If you look at the pictures above, what do you see?

b. Match the different methods of order picking to the pictures and describe them. Use the information in the text above and the words in the word bank from page 83.

81

4 Order Picking and Packing Goods

c. Which method(s) do you use in your company? Explain to the class.

4.1 Order Picking

4.1.1 VOCABULARY WORK

Find words in the box below which fit these definitions or explanations.

customer | labour-intensive | order picker | order picking | supply chain | warehouse

1. extracting goods

2. person who extracts goods from a warehousing system

3. way from producer to the customer

4. to whom goods are delivered

5. where goods are stored

6. is a lot of work

Order Picking and Packing Goods

4.1.2 DISCUSSION

To what extent will order picking be possible without the help of manpower in the future? Use the words in the word bank. Before starting a class discussion, collect useful phrases like "in my opinion" or "on the one hand" etc. on the board.

WORD BANK

to become redundant	seinen Arbeitsplatz verlieren
(electronic) order picking	(beleglose) Kommissionierung
to decrease	fallen
to facilitate	erleichtern
to increase	steigen
logistics	Versorgung, Logistik
low level order picking	maschinengestützte Kommissionierung
pick-by-barcode	Kommisionieren per Strichcode
pick-by-light	Kommisionieren per LED-Anzeigen
pick-by-vision	Kommissionieren per Datenbrille
pick-by-voice	Kommissionieren per Sprachbefehl
order picking by pick list	beleghafte Kommissionierung
time-consuming	zeitaufwändig

4.1.3 MATCHING

We can identify five main types of order picking. Match them with the definitions.

1. **picker to part method**
2. **sorting systems method**
3. **pick to box method**
4. **zone picking method**
5. **wave picking method**

a. Each order picker is assigned to one specific zone.
b. The order picker moves to collect the products necessary for several orders.
c. No movement of the order picker, the picking area is organised so that there are a number of picking stations connected by a conveyor. The order picker fills the box with the products from his station and the box moves to the other picking stations until the customer's order is complete.
d. The order picker moves to collect the products necessary for one order.
e. No movement of the order picker, the products are brought to him/her by an automatic system.

Order Picking and Packing Goods

4.1.4 CREATIVE ACTIVITY

Chart a workflow of the "sorting systems method" and the "zone picking method" in your exercise book.

Order Picking and Packing Goods

4.1.5 WRITING

What are the in-house and external reasons for extracting goods from a warehousing system? Match the pictures above with the keywords below and build complete sentences.

- sold out: *The warehouse assistant extracts goods because the products are sold out.*
- annual stocktaking:
- new product line:
- seasonal sales:
- assembly line:

4.1.6 READING

Read the text carefully and decide if the statements below are true or false.

Cold storage warehouse fire strategy

While it may seem counterintuitive that fire is even a risk in spaces designed to maintain cold temperatures, cold storage in fact presents a huge fire hazard for warehouse designers and builders, life safety installation companies and facility owners. [...]

From a feasibility point of view [...], cold storage is substantially more complicated and more
5 expensive than dry storage because of the regulations around refrigerated freight. Plus, the very nature of the materials used in cold storage, means it presents a higher risk factor when it comes to fire. So as the demand for refrigerated products grows, so does the need for better fire safety. [...]

Dangerous scenarios are preventable when fire safety experts have been consulted, the cor-
10 rect life safety equipment is installed, the electrics and mechanical devices in use within the building are well serviced and the correct health and safety regulations are followed. Essential action when you consider preventable fires in the UK warehouse industry costs our economy upwards of £230 billion each year. [...]

Source: Cold storage warehouse fire strategy, in: LogisticsHandling.com. International Resource for Material Handling & Logistics. https://www.logisticshandling.com/articles/2023/02/07/cold-storage-warehouse-fire-strategy/ [07.03.2023]

Order Picking and Packing Goods

TRUE (=T) OR FALSE (=F)

☐ 1. Fire is no risk in spaces of cold temperature.

☐ 2. Cold storage presents a fire hazard only for warehouse designers.

☐ 3. Cold storage is more complicated than dry storage.

☐ 4. Only fire protection experts are needed to prevent dangerous scenarios.

☐ 5. Better fire safety grows with the demand for refrigerated products.

☐ 6. Preventable fires cost £230 billion each month.

WORD BANK	
cold storage	Kühllager
counterintuitive	widersinnig
fire hazard	Brandgefahr
feasibility	Machbarkeit
refrigerated freight	Kühltransport
demand	Nachfrage
fire safety	Brandschutz
safety equipment	Sicherheitsausrüstung
safety regulations	Sicherheitsvorschriften
to prevent	vermeiden
warehouse industry	Lagerbranche
economy	Wirtschaft
billion	Milliarde

4.1.7 WRITING

Find a subheading for each of the three paragraphs in the text "Cold storage warehouse fire strategy" on page 85. Hide your three subheadings in a word field like the one on page 41. Make your neighbour find them.

4.1.8 MEDIATION

Your colleague doesn't understand English very well and asks you to summarise "Cold storage warehouse fire strategy".
Read the text again and make notes of the important points. Then write a short summary in German.

Order Picking and Packing Goods

4.2 Packing Goods

4.2.1 VOCABULARY

Match the types of packing to the pictures.

barrel | bottle | cardboard box | container | pallet | sack

4.2.2 READING

Read the text and find the English equivalents of some highlighted terms.

Packaging
Packaging can be described as a coordinated system of preparing goods for transport, warehousing, logistics, sale and end use. Packaging contains, protects, preserves, informs, sells and makes transport safe.

Suitable packaging of a product is a critical factor in logistics. Without it, many logistics pro-
5 cesses could not be performed at all or could be carried out only at great additional cost. The function of packaging is not just to protect the product from mechanical or climatic stresses during delivery. It affects many other jobs.

These include providing information about the contents as well as enabling and facilitating transport, handling, storage and order picking. Packaging can have features that add conveni-
10 ence in distribution, handling, stacking, display, sale, opening, reclosing, use, dispensing and reuse. The packaging and labels can be used by marketers to encourage potential buyers to purchase the product at the point of sale.

Etikett		Verkauf	
schützen		Lagerung	
Verbraucher-freundlichkeit		kaufen	
konservieren		Auslieferung	

4.2.3 VOCABULARY

Find words in the text above which fit these definitions or explanations.

1. protects from mechanical stress
2. transport goods from one place to another
3. is inside the packaging
4. where goods are sold
5. are used by marketers to encourage buyers
6. the state of being useful, functional and advantageous
7. cannot be performed without packaging

4.2.4 READING

Read the text once more. Say whether the statements are true or false. Correct the false ones.

TRUE (=T) OR FALSE (=F)

☐ 1. Packaging is an uncoordinated system.

☐ 2. Without packaging many logistics processes could be carried out at low cost.

☐ 3. Packaging protects the product during delivery.

☐ 4. Packaging enables storage.

☐ 5. Packaging can be used by customers to sell the product.

4.2.5 MATCHING

Match the English words and phrases with the German equivalents.

☐ 1. adhesive tape   a. Füllmittel
☐ 2. bubble bag   b. zerbrechlich
☐ 3. corrugated board   c. Packmittel
☐ 5. filling material   d. Klebe-/Packband
☐ 6. fragile   e. vor Nässe schützen
☐ 7. to keep dry   f. Luftkissenpolster
☐ 8. package   g. Mehrwegpalette
☐ 9. packing material   h. Stapelbehälter
☐ 10. point of sale   i. Packstück
☐ 11. returnable pallet   j. Verkaufsplatz/-stelle
☐ 12. stackable bin   k. Wellpappe

4.2.6 DISCUSSION

Why is it important to have different types of packaging? Discuss in small groups. Make notes and present your results to the class. Use the vocabulary from exercise 4.2.5.

SKILLS

If you have to hold a presentation, the following tips might be useful for you:
1. Inform yourself about the topic of the presentation carefully.
2. Think about the way you want to present your topic.
3. Make sure that the technical equipment is available and in good condition.
4. Only write notes and speak freely to the class.
5. Prepare yourself for questions and have further information at hand.
6. Try to keep eye contact with the class and the teacher.

4 Order Picking and Packing Goods

4.2.7 MATCHING

Which type(s) of packing is (are) suitable for each item?

4.2.8 READING

a. Read the interview and answer the following questions about what Johannes Küstner, head of National Road Transport | Environment at DSLV (Federal Association of Freight Forwarding and Logistics) is talking about.

How can the transformation to CO_2-free road freight transport succeed?

What "tools" does the logistics industry need to provide CO_2-free services?

The freight forwarding industry is, of course, fundamentally capable of action. Through continuous optimisation of logistical processes, it already makes a decisive contribution to
5 avoiding traffic and thus to reducing emissions. This also includes the growing inclusion of rail and inland waterways in supply chains. Logistics can develop and strengthen its organisational competence even further, especially with the help of digitalisation.

The logistics sector has also already significantly reduced specific CO_2 emissions. However, in recent years it has been overtaken by its own success, because the absolute CO_2
10 emissions of freight transport have steadily increased due to the constant rise in transport performance of all modes of transport. The logistics sector can therefore only contribute to the internationally agreed CO_2 reduction targets, to which it is expressly committed, with the help of a fundamental change in alternative vehicle and drive technologies as well as post-fossil energies. For this, it needs the support of the manufacturing industry and the
15 energy sector. [...]

Order Picking and Packing Goods

Which alternative drive technologies will logistics use in the future?

A mix of technologies can be assumed. For urban and regional transport, battery electric vehicles (BEVs) will probably prevail; for longer distances, hydrogen trucks are likely to be used according to the current status, although BEVs could also be used here in the medium term. The BMVI also includes trolley trucks in its overall concept. However, these will probably only have a limited radius of use on selected routes between industrial and commercial centres and ports. It will be rather difficult to set up a European overhead line infrastructure for this. However, dynamic charging via overhead lines remains an interesting option. The production of renewable electricity or hydrogen and the standardised development of a Europe-wide refuelling and charging infrastructure remain crucial for the climate-neutral use of alternative technologies. The energy industry must play an active role here.

[...]

Will the Fuel Emission Trading Act (BEHG) accelerate the decarbonisation of road freight transport?

This is not to be expected for the time being. This is because the politically intended steering effect will not occur immediately, as there are no alternative drive systems for long-distance transport that are ready for series production and the railways still need years to be upgraded. As a result, the emissions trading system will initially only become an additional cost burden and will rather deprive the freight forwarding industry of investment reserves for the future acquisition of a fleet of vehicles with alternative drives. The Fuel Emission Trading Act (BEHG), as the implementing law for national emissions trading, increased the price of diesel by up to 8 ct/litre as early as 1 January 2021. This means on average up to 2,500 euros higher operating costs per truck in 2021. The environment will not benefit from this for the time being.

Source: Bundesverband Spedition und Logistik (DSLV): Fünf Fragen an ... Johannes Küstner, Leiter Nationaler Straßengüterverkehr. Wie gelingt die Transformation zum CO_2-freien Straßengüterverkehr?, 26.11.2020, www.dslv.org/de/aktuelles/meldung/wie-gelingt-die-transformation-zum-co2-freien-strassengueterverkehr (translated by Thomas Meinen) [07.11.2022]

b. Decide whether the following statements are true. Tick (✓) the correct answer.

☐ 1. Logistics can develop its organisational competence even further without the help of digitalisation.

☐ 2. The logistics sector has also already significantly reduced specific CO_2 emissions.

☐ 3. For urban and regional transport, battery electric vehicles (BEVs) will probably prevail.

☐ 4. The BMVI does not include trolley trucks in its overall concept.

☐ 5. The production of renewable electricity or hydrogen remains crucial for the climate-neutral use of alternative technologies.

☐ 6. The politically desired steering effect can be achieved immediately, as there are alternative drives for long-distance traffic that are ready for series production.

☐ 7. This was on average up to 5,000 euros higher operating costs per truck in 2021.

Order Picking and Packing Goods

c. Answer the following questions on the text in complete sentences.

1. How does the logistics sector contribute to reducing CO_2 emissions?

2. Which drive technologies will prevail in the future?

3. How much higher were the operating costs per truck in 2021?

d. Find the following statements in the text and write them down in English.

1. Durch kontinuierliche Optimierung der logistischen Prozesse trägt sie selbst bereits entscheidend zur Verkehrsvermeidung und damit zur Emissionsreduzierung bei.

2. Die Logistikbranche hat die spezifischen CO_2-Emissionen auch bereits deutlich verringert.

3. Für urbane und regionale Verkehre werden sich wohl batterieelektrische Fahrzeuge (BEV) durchsetzen.

4.2.9 MEDIATION

You started an apprenticeship working in a logistics company whose head office is in Great Britain. It has been a fantastic experience for you. Your friend is also interested in starting an apprenticeship in logistics next year and wants to ask the Human Resources Manager, Mr Clark, who speaks only English, some questions. Unfortunately, your friend doesn't speak English very well and asks you for help.

Mediate between the conversation partners.

Your friend: Hallo Mr Clark, ich möchte im nächsten Jahr gerne eine Ausbildung in Ihrem Unternehmen beginnen. Welche Unterlagen benötigen Sie?

You:

Order Picking and Packing Goods

4

Mr Clark: First of all, I am glad to hear that. Our company is always in search of young talents. To answer your question, we need a curriculum vitae and a meaningful cover letter from him/her.

You:

Your friend: Ich möchte wissen, wie lange eine Ausbildung dauert.

You:

Mr Clark: The training usually lasts three years.

You:

Your friend: Frag ihn bitte, welchen Schulabschluss ich benötige.

You:

Mr Clark: It depends on what you want to become. To work as a specialist for warehouse logistics you need a secondary school leaving certificate. If you want to become a freight forwarding and logistics services clerk, you'll need at least a secondary school leaving certificate and a good knowledge of English.

You:

Your friend: Ich fürchte, dass ich meine Englischkenntnisse noch verbessern muss. Dann werde ich mich aber auf jeden Fall noch einmal bewerben. Vielen Dank für die Auskünfte und bis bald.

You:

Mr Clark: No problem, you're welcome.

4.2.10 REPORTED SPEECH

Corresponding to the Mediation above, here are some sentences in direct speech. Change them into reported speech.

1. Henry: "My wife **is** at home."

2. Sheila: "My friend often **reads** a book."

3. Sandra: "I'**m** watering the flowers."

Order Picking and Packing Goods

4. Archie: "My brother **was** ill."

5. Rupert: "I **am going to** ride my bike."

6. Simon and Claire: "We **have cleaned** our room."

7. Charles: "I **didn't have** time to clean the windows."

8. Sherlock Holmes: "My friend Watson **will be** 60 years old."

9. James: "The boss **must** sign the contract."

10. Patricia: "My husband **helped** in the house."

WORD BANK	
to provide	bereitstellen, anbieten
freight forwarding industry	Speditionsbranche
to reduce	verringern
drive technology	Antriebstechnologie
hydrogen	Wasserstoff
decarbonisation	Reduzierung von CO_2-Emissionen
to accelerate	beschleunigen
to intend	beabsichtigen, anstreben
steering	Lenkung, Steuerung
additional	zusätzlich
average	Durchschnitt
apprenticeship	Ausbildung
curriculum vitae	Lebenslauf

4.2.11 GROUP WORK

Think about order picking and packaging in the future and present your ideas to the class. Use the following terms (translate first).

environment   sustainability

energy   waste

responsible   economic

Order Picking and Packing Goods

4.2.12 WRITING

Comment on the following statement by a marketer. Write 80 to 100 words.

"The main purpose of packaging is to sell the product and not to save the environment."

HOW TO USE

Word Order

Wortstellung in Aussagesätzen:
– normale Wortstellung:
  Subjekt (wer)   Verb (macht)   Objekt (was)
  I   pick   orders.
  The teacher   speaks   English.
 	
Wortstellung in Fragen:
– ist das Fragewort Subjekt, gilt die normale Worstellung:
  Subjekt (wer)   Verb (macht)   Objekt (was)
  Who   is reading   the book?
 	
– in allen anderen Fällen wird ein Hilfsverb verwendet:
  Objekt   Hilfsverb   Subjekt   Verb
  What   did   you   see?

Achtung:	
– in Nebensätzen bleibt diese Wortstellung immer erhalten	I always finish at five o'clock because **my train leaves the station** at half past five.
– Adverbien der Häufigkeit, die aus einem Wort bestehen, z. B. usually, sometimes etc., stehen vor dem (Voll-)Verb	I **always** pick the new orders.
– Adverbien der Häufigkeit, die aus mehreren Wörtern bestehen, z. B. this week, every day etc., stehen am Satzende	I unload the lorries **every morning**.

4.2.13 EXERCISE

a. Form sentences with the words below. Note the correct word order.

1. tea / drinks / my mother / every afternoon

2. can not / English / understand / he

3. brought / me / the postman / a letter

4. broke / the glasses / who

5. where / buy / this book / did / you

6. he / why / did / late / come

7. the train / here / comes

8. work / at seven o'clock / I / in the morning / start

9. over the fence / into the garden / the cat / jumped

10. Jeremy / a kiss / yesterday / Helen / gave

b. Form questions out of sentences 7 to 10 in exercise a.

1. the train / here / comes

Order Picking and Packing Goods

2. work / at seven o'clock / I / in the morning / start

3. over the fence / into the garden / the cat / jumped

4. Jeremy / a kiss / yesterday / Helen / gave

HOW TO USE

Adjectives and Adverbs	
Anwendung:	
Adjektive beschreiben das Substantiv näher. Sie stehen entweder vor dem Substantiv oder nach dem Verb „to be".	I like **interesting** work. My work is **interesting**.
Adverbien beschreiben, wie jemand etwas tut oder wie etwas geschieht. Sie bestimmen Verben, Adjektive oder andere Adverbien näher.	He drives the forklift **carefully**. (Bezug auf das Verb) Ronald is **extremely** clever at picking goods. (Bezug auf das Adjektiv) Diana learns warning signs **extremely** quickly. (Bezug auf das Adverb)
Bildung von Adverbien: Adverb = Adjektiv + „-ly"	
Achtung: – endet das Adjektiv auf „y", verwandelt sich dieses in ein „i", z. B. happy – happily, easy – easily – einige Adverbien haben die gleiche Form wie das Adjektiv, z. B. hard – hard, late – late, fast – fast – einige Wörter sehen aus wie Adverbien, haben aber eine andere Bedeutung, z. B. hardly (kaum), lately (kürzlich, neulich)	

4.2.14 WRITING

Fill in the correct form of the adjective or adverb.

He is a very (1) _____ (reliable) worker.

The secretary works on the computer (2) _____ (efficient).

I should learn my vocabulary more (3) _____ (precise).

We have (4) _____ (regular) meetings with all the team members.

I was able to buy this machine quite (5) _____ (cheap).

Yesterday, we had a very (6) _____ (funny) situation at work.

My teacher was very (7) _____ (angry) with me because I had forgotten my homework.

He shouted at me (8) _____ (angry).

My new job is very (9) _____ (interesting).

I looked at the new girl in my class (10) _____ (curious).

4.2.15 EXERCISE

Describe your job, your workplace and your working environment in five sentences with adjectives.

Example: *I work at a big warehouse.*

1.
2.
3.
4.
5.

4.2.16 EXERCISE

Describe how your boss and your colleagues do things using five adverbs.

Example: *My colleague Peter drives the forklift recklessly.*

1.
2.
3.
4.
5.

Order Picking and Packing Goods

4.3 Business Correspondence – Orders

4.3.1 MATCHING

Study the chart of the Incoterms® 2020*. Then complete the tables below using the words in the box.

Incoterms® 2020

The Incoterms® 2020 (international commercial terms) are determined by the International Chamber of Commerce. They help facilitate the understanding of delivery terms in international trade. The Incoterms® 2020 are the revised form of Incoterms® 2010 and came into force on 1 January 2020. They contain the following set of terms:

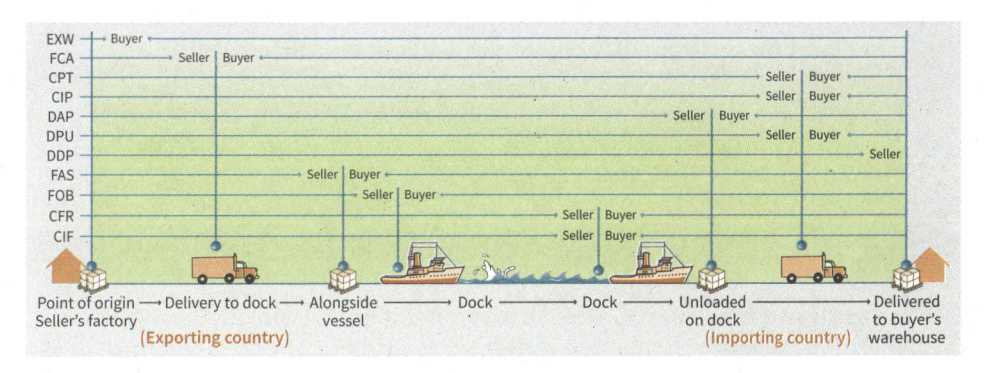

> ab Werk | carriage and insurance paid to | cost, insurance and freight | CPT | DAP | delivered duty paid | FOB | free carrier | frei Längsseite Schiff | Kosten und Fracht

Incoterms® 2020 applicable for all modes of transport

EXW	ex works	named place	
FCA		named place	frei Frachtführer
	carriage paid to	named place of destination	frachtfrei
CIP		named place of destination	frachtfrei, versichert
	delivered at place	named place	geliefert benannter Ort
DPU	delivered at place unloaded	named place	geliefert benannter Ort entladen
DDP		named place of destination	geliefert verzollt

---

* Für die Nutzung der Incoterms® in einem Vertrag empfiehlt sich die Bezugnahme auf den Originaltext des Regelwerks. „Incoterms®" ist eine eingetragene Marke der Internationalen Handelskammer (ICC). Incoterms® 2020 ist einschließlich aller seiner Teile urheberrechtlich geschützt. Die ICC ist Inhaberin der Urheberrechte an den Incoterms® 2020. Bei den vorliegenden Ausführungen handelt es sich um inhaltliche Interpretationen zu den von der ICC herausgegebenen Lieferbedingungen durch die Autoren. Diese sind für den Inhalt, Formulierungen und Grafiken in dieser Veröffentlichung verantwortlich. Der Originaltext kann über ICC Germany unter www.iccgermany.de und www.incoterms2020.de bezogen werden.

Order Picking and Packing Goods

4

Incoterms® 2020 only applicable for sea and inland waterway transport

FAS	free alongside ship	named port of shipment	
	free on board	named port of shipment	frei an Bord
CFR	cost and freight	named port of destination	
CIF		named port of destination	Kosten, Versicherung u. Fracht

4.3.2 READING

Read the text and circle the correct words in the shaded fields.

Orders are replies *to/for* formal offers. They are often placed by sending a letter, e-mail or fax *to/at* the supplier. Many companies use a preprinted order or purchase order form *which/who* contains blank spaces. This form has to be filled *in/up* by the buyer, giving the required details an order should contain. Nevertheless, it is still common practice to order goods *with/by* sending a letter, fax or e-mail. Regarding faxes, there is no specific form or layout. Companies may design their individual layout *for/about* fax transmissions.

4.3.3 ANALYSING

Put the jumbled parts of the following fax order into the right order. Use the numbers 1 to 9.

20–OCT–20..   14:43 PM   010789650   1/1

SHAMROCK & HARPER LOGISTICS
Kingswood Business Park – Dublin 22
Phone: 010789654   Fax: 010789650   E-mail: shamrock@s&h.ie

To:	Tom Branson	Date:	20 October 20..
	Harkley Lifting Ltd.	Subject:	Order No. 1456
From:	Flore Kenmoe	Pages:	1

We look forward to receiving your confirmation of this order soon.

Many thanks for your offer of 6 September 20...

As we are in urgent need of the ordered items, we would appreciate delivery by 15 November at the latest.

Quantity	Item No.	Description	Unit price	Total
10	3310	Heavy Duty Ratchet Strap	€ 14.50	€ 145.00
15	6610	Auto Ratchet Strap 1,8 mtr.	€ 15.00	€ 225.00
20	6680	Auto Rachet Strap 3 mtr.	€ 19.00	€ 380.00

Prices are quoted free domicile, exclusive of VAT, payable at 30 days net, 14 days 2%.

Order Picking and Packing Goods

4

>Yours sincerely
>*Flore Kenmoe*
>Flore Kenmoe
>Purchasing

>We have studied your quotation and find the offered ratchet straps satisfactory. Therefore, we take pleasure in ordering as follows:

>Dear Mr Branson

4.3.4 ANALYSING

You work for *ABC Storage Ltd*. 21/24 Broom Road, Bristol BS4 5RG. The company wants to expand the storage capacity of its warehouse.

Study the quotation from *Bakker-Plast BV* and your forwarding agent's pricelist. Use the calculation form below to find out the most favourable price. Then order 200 pallet boxes, item no. 40-10202.

From	bakker@plast.nl
To	morton@abc.co.uk
Date	10 October 20..
Subject	Enquiry for pallet boxes

Dear Mr Morton

Quotation No. 7802/jh

Thank you very much for your message and your interest in our pallets.

We would now like to submit the following quotation:

Item no. 40-10202 – Plastic Pallet Box L 202
Dimensions 1200x1000x750 mm – volume 616 litres – max load per box 450 kg
EXW   £245.00
FOB Rotterdam   £305.00
CIF Southampton   £375.00

Prices are to be understood inclusive of VAT.
On orders over 150 units we can grant a 10 % quantity discount.
Terms of payment: 30 days net, 10 days 2 %.
Delivery can be effected within 10 days from receipt of order.

We look forward to welcoming you as a new customer.

Yours sincerely
Jan Holst
Bakker-Plast BV * Sontplein 10 * 9723 BZ Groningen
Phone: 0031(0)6689-124589 * Fax: 0031(0)6689-124580

McPherson Transport and Haulage

PRICELIST

Sea carriage	£65
Road transport Southampton – Bristol	£25
Road transport Groningen – Rotterdam	£45

Order Picking and Packing Goods

CALCULATION FORM

Delivery Term	Price Bakker Plast	Road Groningen-Rotterdam	Sea carriage	Road Southampton-Bristol	Total
EXW	£245	£45	£65	£25	£380*
FOB					
CIF					

* most favourable price

4.3.5 WRITING

Use the order form and place the order according to your price calculation in exercise 4.3.4.

PURCHASE ORDER FORM
⇨ Fax 0031(0)6689 – 124589 ⇨ Phone 0031(0)6689 – 124580

Bakker-Plast B.V., Sontplein 10, 9723 BZ Groningen

Sender/invoice recipient

Order No.: _____ .   as per quotation No. _____

Code No.	Item	QTY	Unit price £	Total £
			Subtotal	
			Less discount 10 %	
			Grand Total £	

Please select your mode of transport
EXW ☐   FOB Rotterdam ☐   CIF Southampton ☐

Signature: _____   Date: _____

Order Picking and Packing Goods

4.3.6 MATCHING

From	Jesse.Smith@deltafood.co.uk
To	John.MacSwift@galaton.co.uk
Date	12 February 20..
Subject	Your offer for ear plugs and special offer for smoke detectors
Attachments:	Purchase order No. 127609

Dear Mr MacSwift

Thank you for your offer of 10 February 20.. — **1 Referring to former contact**

We have studied your offer for adjustable ear plugs carefully and find your conditions satisfactory. — **2 Articles you want to order**

We would also like to take advantage of your special offer for smoke detectors.

Attached, we are sending you our purchase order No. 127609 amounting to a total of £950.00.

As we are in urgent need of the items, it is absolutely essential that the articles arrive at our warehouse by 20 February 20.. — **3 Terms of delivery**

Please note that all goods are to be delivered to our branch at 37 Garden Avenue, Uxbridge UB8 1SA.

Payment will be effected as per your offer 30 days net. — **4 Terms of payment**

We look forward to receiving the goods in time. — **5 Closing**

Yours sincerely

Jesse Smith
Deltafood, 62 High Street, Nottingham N62 1GW
Phone 01234 5678
www.deltafood.co.uk

Match the sentences a–h to the structuring elements of orders 1–5 below.
a. Thank you for your e-mail of 7 March quoting prices for the super pallets PA59.
b. Please deliver as per the conditions stated in your offer of 3 August.
c. Prices are to be understood ex works.
d. We have studied your offer No. 95223 of 10 March and would now like to order as follows.
e. Could you please make sure that the articles will reach us by 9 March at the latest.
f. Please send us the following articles as per your quotation of 7 June.
g. Payment will be made on the basis of 14 days net after the date of invoice.
h. We look forward to receiving your order confirmation.

Order Picking and Packing Goods

Structuring elements of orders

1 Referring to former contact

2 Articles you want to order

3 Terms of delivery

4 Terms of payment

5 Closing

4.3.7 WRITING

You are Sarah Lee. You work for Galaton, Newcastle. You have received a quotation from John Manson of Hot & Black.

Please order for the staff bistro 15 kg of item No. 3125 and 5 kg of item No. 6710.
Write an e-mail to j.manson@hotandblack.co.uk.
You need the coffee within 5 days as stock is running low. The coffee is to be delivered to the staff bistro at 37 Garden Avenue.

We appreciate your interest in our quality coffee.
We take pleasure in submitting the following quotation:

Item No.	Description	£ per kilo
3125	*Apollo* smooth medium bodied, sweet, chocolaty-nutty aroma, touch of acidity	7.00
4104	*Luna* intense, full bodied, bitter chocolate aroma, smoky aftertaste	8.00
6710	**Decaffeinated** delicate with some sweetness, citrus fruit and roasted flavour	7.70

Order Picking and Packing Goods

4

Please note that our prices are to be understood inclusive of VAT. We offer a quantity discount of 10 % off the prices quoted for orders over 30 kg.
Delivery can be effected within 5–8 days after receipt of your order.
Our usual terms of payment are 30 days net.
We hope this quotation comes up to your expectations and look forward to hearing from you.
Yours sincerely

From	Sarah.Lee@galaton.co.uk
To	
Date	
Subject	

Dear Mr Manson
Order No. 12345

Quantity	Item No.	Description	£ per kilo	Total

Subtotal

Total

Yours sincerely

WORD BANK

confirmation	Bestätigung
to effect payment	eine Zahlung leisten
free domicile	frei Haus
quotation	Preisangebot
recipient	Abnehmer, Empfänger
storage capacity	Lagerkapazität

4.3.8 CROSSWORD

Fill in the English translation of the words below.

DOWN
1. Lieferkette
2. Lagerhalle
3. Inventur
4. Gang
5. kommissionieren
6. Nachhaltigkeit
7. schützen
8. ausverkauft
9. Etikett
10. Kollege/Kollegin
11. Einlagerung

ACROSS
12. Kunde
13. Packmittel
14. Verkaufsplatz
15. zerbrechlich
16. Umwelt
17. Fließband
18. Haltbarkeit
19. Fass
20. Verbraucherfreundlichkeit

5 Transport and Logistics

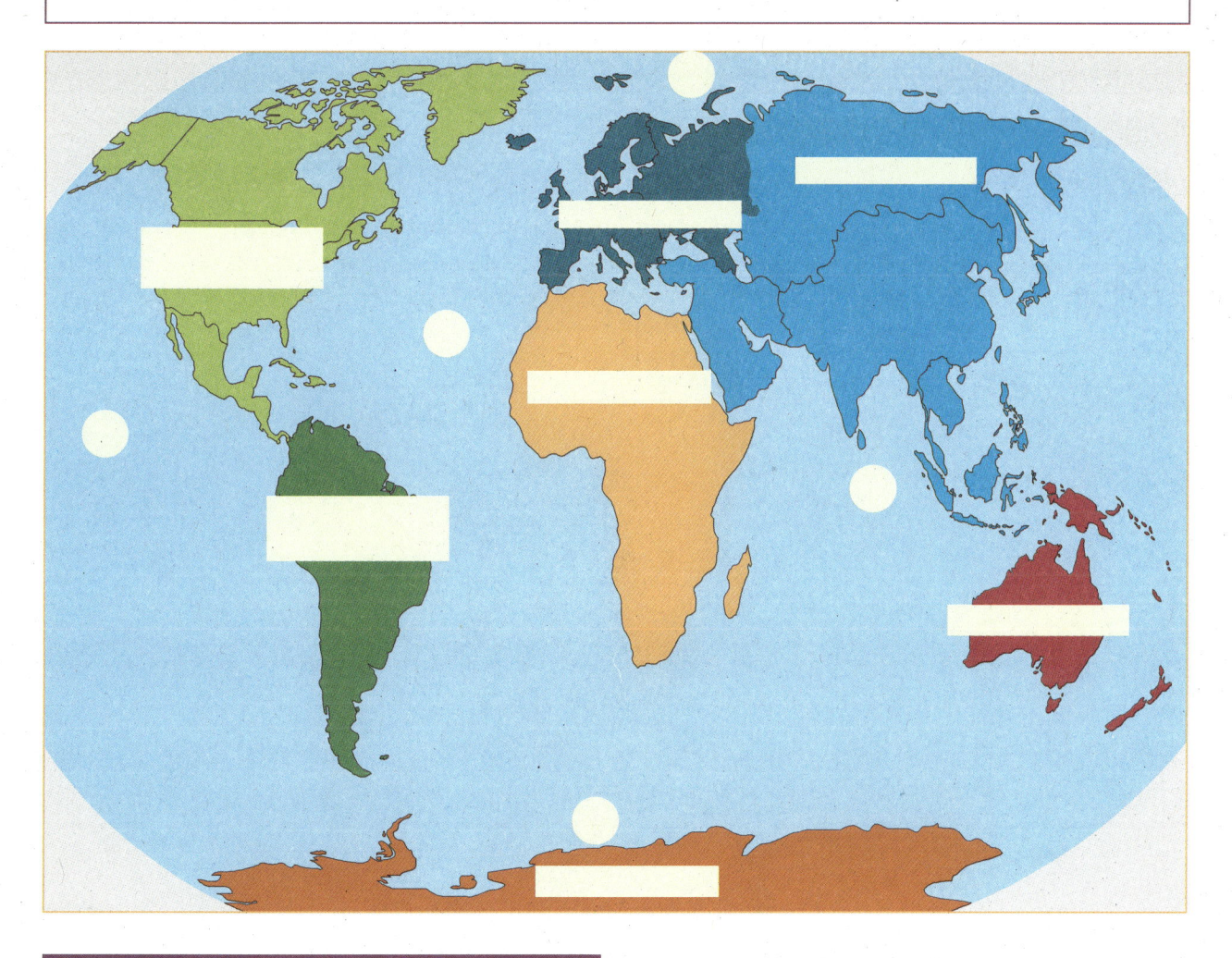

ANALYSING

Mark on the world map:
- the seven most commonly recognised continents
- the five oceans: Pacific Ocean (a.), Atlantic Ocean (b.), Indian Ocean (c.), Antarctic Ocean (d.), Arctic Ocean (e.).
- the world's five largest economies in terms of the GDP (Gross Domestic Product)

- countries you do business with (customers or suppliers)

SKILLS

Capitalisation in written English
In order to avoid unnecessary mistakes, obey these three capitalisation rules:
1. We capitalise the first letter at the beginning of a new sentence.
2. The pronoun 'I' is always capitalised.
3. Proper names are capitalised, e. g.:
    - personal names (Elisabeth)
    - names of companies, institutions, brands etc. (the Scottish Parliament)
    - names of cities, countries, continents and geographical terms (London, Spain, Africa, the River Thames)
    - months, days of the week, bank holidays (June, Saturday, Christmas)

Transport and Logistics

5.1 European Countries

5.1.1 MATCHING

Name the European countries from 1 to 31 on the map of Europe. Complete the table in your exercise book by using the table below.

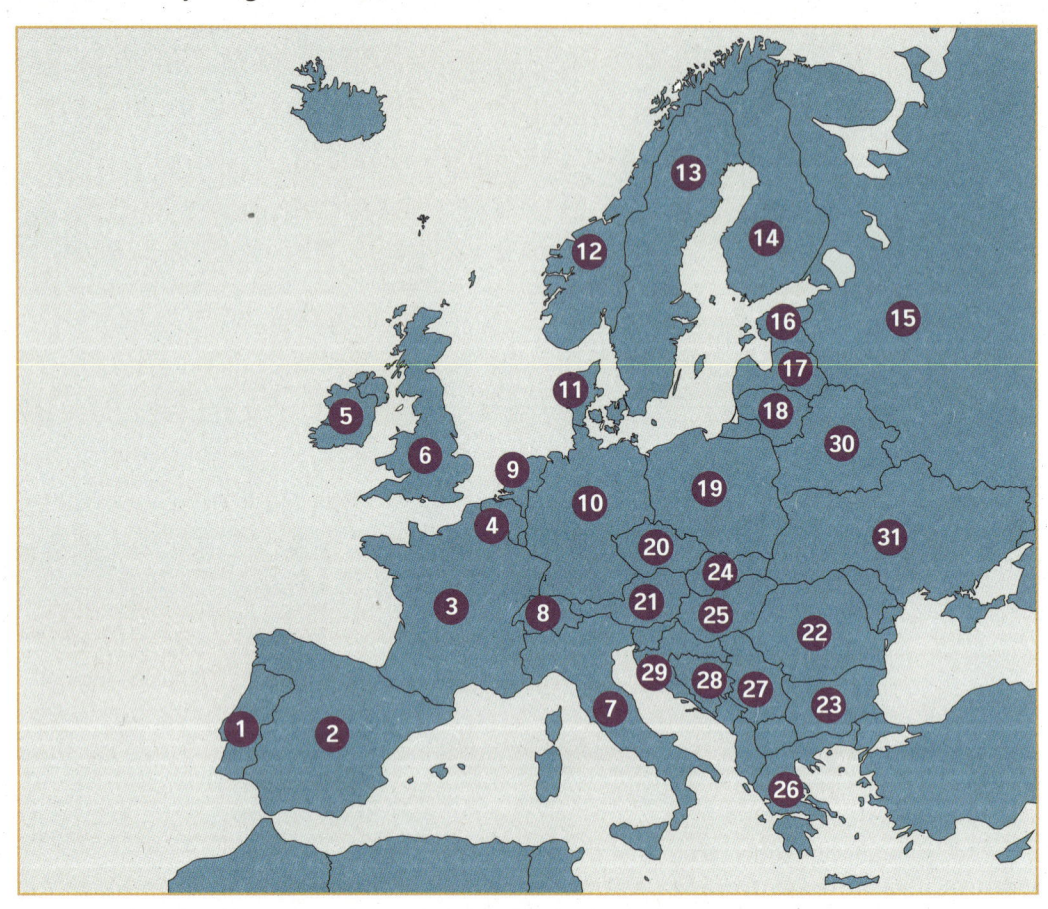

	Country	Capital	Language	Currency
1				
2				
3				
4				
5				
6				

Transport and Logistics 5

	Country	Capital	Language	Currency
7				
8				
9				
10				
11				
12				
13				
14				
15				
16				
17				
18				
19				
20				
21				
22				
23				
24				
25				
26				
27				
28				
29				
30				
31				

Transport and Logistics

5.2 Organising a Transport

5.2.1 BRAINSTORMING

Your colleague Paul, who is normally in charge of planning routes for the international trade, has become seriously ill. Your manager, Mike Smith, wants you to organise a transport from Hamburg to Hong Kong in China. What do you have to keep in mind if you want to make the transport a success? Use a mind map for collecting your ideas.

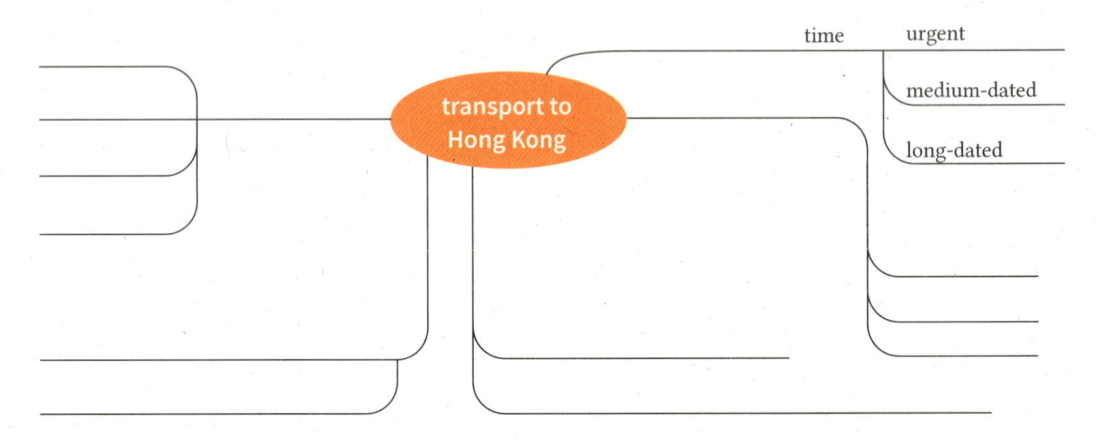

Mind map centred on "transport to Hong Kong" with branch "time" containing: urgent, medium-dated, long-dated.

5.2.2 READING

Read the e-mail from Mike Smith and complete the text with words from the box.

| condition | costs | customer | mode of transport | route | screws | urgently | warehouse |

Von: Mike.smith@yahoo.com
An:
Datum:
Betreff:

Hi Sarah,

In general, organising a transport requires a lot of individual knowledge and a whole bunch of aspects that have to be taken into consideration. Your job is to bring the customer needs and your internal **workflow** together.

Before the goods leave the (1) _____ for China, a couple of questions have to be

answered: When do you have to send the consignment so that the (2) _____ gets it on time? It is rather obvious that this information is needed in order to decide which

(3) _____ you choose.

Imagine your client needs the goods (4) _____ and you decide to send them by ship! That leads you to another important question: Which mode of transport fits best for the goods you are going to transport? I am sure you agree that there is a difference whether you just send a packet of

110

(5) _____, a pallet packed with fragile glass or 200 tons of bulk cargo. Moreover, you should also think about how to pack your goods so that they arrive at the buyer's premises in perfect (6) _____. The decision on appropriate packing material is closely related to safety aspects. Ignoring that can cause much trouble and additional (7) _____ for the sender.

Finally, whenever you plan a (8) _____ and the right mode of transport, you need to think about what (environmental) costs are involved when sending goods. I do hope this is helpful.

Best regards
Mike

5.2.3 MATCHING

a. See whether the contents of the e-mail correspond in any way with your ideas in your mind-map. Compile a list with the major issues you have to bear in mind.

b. Match the highlighted terms in the text with the German equivalents in the box.

> Arbeitsablauf | Lieferung | Palette | passen | Räumlichkeiten | Schüttgut | Versender | verursachen | zerbrechlich

1. _____ _____
2. _____ _____
3. _____ _____
4. _____ _____
5. _____ _____
6. _____ _____
7. _____ _____
8. _____ _____
9. _____ _____

5 Transport and Logistics

5.3 Going Global

5.3.1 SURVEY

a. Read the following quotations of warehouse logistics operators. Which one do you most agree with?

b. Work in small groups. Create questions for a questionnaire and present it to the class.

c. Ask three to five colleagues and report to the class next week.

> "People say globalisation is bad for jobs in Germany because many companies shift their production to low-wage countries."

> "I do not care about globalisation. Our company is too small to take part in global trade."

> "Globalisation has turned the world into a huge toy shop with every one of us as potential seller and buyer."

> "20 years ago we did business nationwide or with companies in Austria, Switzerland, Belgium or the Netherlands. Nowadays, we receive containers from China, consignments from Brazil or India and we send off goods to Korea."

5.3.2 READING

Read the article and number the paragraphs in the correct order 1 to 5. Then answer the questions below.

The Features of Globalisation

[ ] No technology has had such a huge impact on globalisation as the Internet. It **spans** the world and makes it easy to communicate and to do business. **Literally**, everyone can **set up** a business and buy and sell via the Internet.

[ ] In conclusion, whether we want it or not, globalisation greatly affects our lives. You can decide to buy a computer mouse for little more than two euros including shipping or strawberries in wintertime.

[ ] But there are also many negative aspects of globalisation such as the **exploitation** of poor countries and **interdependence**. That means countries **depend on** each other in terms of import and export. Political or economic crises might lead to a **shortage** of goods. Additionally, companies move their production **abroad** or outsource departments. Very often many people lose their jobs.

[ ] Over the decades, global trade between economies has increased enormously. Globalisation in the modern sense is characterised by cheap production and shipping. Multinational companies produce and sell worldwide and have **gained** huge market power.

[ ] Globalisation, often described as a phenomenon of the 21st century, has its **origins** in the fifteenth century, when European merchants started to discover the world and to sell and buy worldwide.

1. Which negative features of globalisation are mentioned?

2. What are some positive aspects of globalisation?

WORD BANK

abroad	Ausland, ins Ausland
to depend on	abhängig sein von
exploitation	Ausbeutung, Ausnutzung
extent	Ausmaß, Umfang
feature	Merkmal
Gross Domestic Product (GDP)	Bruttoinlandsprodukt
interdependence	Abhängigkeit, Wechselbeziehung
literally	wortwörtlich
origin	Ursprung
to outsource	ausgliedern
questionnaire	Fragebogen
to set up	arrangieren
to shift	verlagern
shortage	Mangel
to span	umfassen, umspannen

Transport and Logistics

5.3.3 DISCUSSION

Work in pairs. Discuss one of the negative aspects in 5.3.1 and add further issues.

5.3.4 WRITING

Comment on one of the quotations on page 112, using your own knowledge and ideas.

SKILLS

How to write a discussion
1. Start with a general introduction on the topic and say whether you agree or disagree with the statement.
2. Collect and group your ideas which speak for and against the statement.
3. Make a concluding statement in which you sum up your arguments.

Transport and Logistics

HOW TO USE

Comparison of Adjectives	
Anwendung:	
Adjektive beschreiben Eigenschaften, z. B. fast (schnell). Mithilfe der Steigerung von Adjektiven, z. B. faster (schneller = Komparativ), the fastest (das schnellste = Superlativ), wird ausgedrückt, in welchem Ausmaß eine Eigenschaft vorhanden ist.	A bike is quite **fast**. A car is **faster** than a bike. A train is the **fastest** vehicle.
Bildung: Komparativ = Adjektiv + „-er" Superlativ = Adjektiv + „-est" – Vergleich, Möglichkeit 1: „… -er / more … than …". – Vergleich, Möglichkeit 2: „… (not) as … as …".	The plane is **faster than** the train. Transport by train is **not as** expensive **as** by plane.
Achtung: – endet das Adjektiv auf „e", entfällt dieses bei der Steigerung	large – lar**ger** – larg**est**
– endet das Adjektiv auf „y", verwandelt sich dieses in ein „i"	busy – busier – busiest
– nach einem kurzen Vokal wird ein Konsonant am Ende des Verbs verdoppelt	big – bigger – biggest
– ist das Adjektiv zweisilbig und endet auf -y, -ow, -er oder -le, wird es wie ein einsilbiges Adjektiv gesteigert	happy – happi**er** – happi**est** narrow – narrow**er** – narrow**est** clever – clever**er** – clever**est** gentle – gentl**er** – gentl**est**
– zweisilbige Adjektive, die auf der ersten Silbe betont werden, sowie drei- und mehrsilbige Adjektive und Partizipien werden mit „**more**" und „**most**" bzw. „**less**" und „**least**" gesteigert	expensive – more expensive – most expensive less expensive – least expensive
– Steigerung von good und bad	good – better – best bad – worse – worst

5.3.5 EXERCISE

Fill in the correct form of the words in brackets (comparative or superlative).

1. Our warehouse is (1) _____ (big) than yours.

2. This road is even (2) _____ (narrow) and (3) _____ (dirty) than the last one.

3. English is one of the (4) _____ (easy) languages and Chinese probably the (5) _____ (difficult) language.

4. My colleagues speak English (6) _____ (good) than me.

5. It was the (7) _____ (bad) day in my life.

5 Transport and Logistics

5.4 Modes of Transport

5.4.1 DISCUSSION

Besides human-powered transportation, such as riding a bicycle or watercraft rowing, and animal-powered transportation, such as transport by horses, donkeys, camels or elephants, 21st century logistics is characterised by highly technologised modes of transportation.

Describe the drawing below. Identify the four modes of transport and explain the most common means of transport. Use the grid below.

	Modes of transport			
	by road	by rail	by sea	by air
Means of transport				

5.4.2 LISTENING FOR GIST

Michael Meier works as a warehouse logistics operator for Logistik-Weltweit GmbH in Hamburg, Germany. His company supplies storage technology and services to wholesalers all over Europe. First read through the following statements, then listen to the audio and decide whether the statements are true or false. If they are wrong, correct them.

TRUE (=T) OR FALSE (=F)?

1. Michael has spoken to Pauline before.

2. Pauline wants to speak with Michael about the latest delivery of electronic control units.

Transport and Logistics

☐ 3. You have to keep faulty items in your company and wait for the supplier's directive.

☐ 4. Pauline's customer needs the device urgently.

☐ 5. Logistik-Weltweit GmbH normally sends its goods by rail.

☐ 6. Transport by air is the fastest mode of transport.

☐ 7. Courier services are less reliable than transport by air.

☐ 8. They choose transport by road.

5.4.3 LISTENING FOR DETAIL

First, read through the following sentences in which some words or phrases are missing. Next, listen to the recording again and fill in the boxes.

Pauline: Good morning. My name is Pauline Bernard from Atlor in Calais. I would like to speak to Michael Meier, please.

Michael: (1) _____. Who am I speaking to?
Pauline: This is Pauline Bernard from Atlor.
Michael: Oh, Pauline, nice to speak to you again! (2) _____?
Pauline: Very well, thank you, and you?
Michael: I am fine, thank you. What can I do for you?
Pauline: Michael, we have got a serious problem. One of our biggest (3) _____ needs an electronic control unit for an automated guided vehicle.

It is very (4) _____ and he keeps on asking when we can (5) _____.

Michael: I understand, Pauline. Did you not receive our last (6) _____ with ten of the electronic control units you need now?
Pauline: Yes, we did, but all those units were sold within four days.
Michael: Hmm, so how do we get the devices from Hamburg to Calais

(7) _____?

We normally transport the goods by ship, but I suppose that will take much too long.

Pauline: Exactly. Time is getting short. We do need an alternative.
Michael: What about using the train?

Pauline: Possibly. It is even (8) _____ than a ship but the transport time is 24 hours. We can't keep the customer waiting that long.
Michael: What do you think about sending the devices by air? It is the (9) _____ mode of transport and you will get the delivery (10) _____.

Pauline: I agree with you, but what about the cost? I am sure (11) _____ is less expensive and as (12) _____ as by plane.
Michael: Listen. First, let me check the prices for the plane and for a courier service. I'll call you back (13) _____ I have more information.
Pauline: Thank you, Michael. Speak to you soon.
Michael: Bye, Pauline.

5.4.4 PRESENTATION

Work in small groups. Choose one mode of transport and discuss its advantages and disadvantages. Next, present your results to the class. Each member of the group should prepare a 60-second talk.

	Advantages	Disadvantages
transport by road		
transport by rail		
transport by sea		
transport by air		

5.4.5 ANALYSING

Form sentences in which you compare the different modes of transport. Use the data about the CO_2 emissions and the costs, and the words in the box.

Example: *Transport by rail is cheaper than by road.*

> cheap | dangerous | economical | environmentally friendly | environmentally (un)friendly | expensive | fast | flexible | quick | reliable | risky | safe | secure | slow | time-consuming

Transport and Logistics

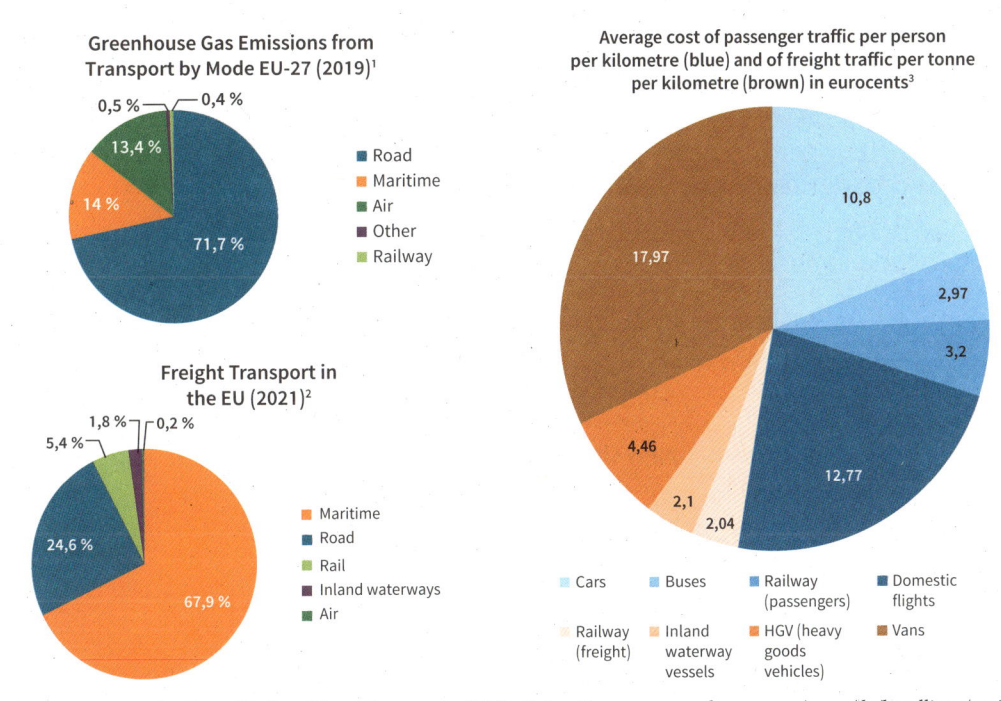

Greenhouse Gas Emissions from Transport by Mode EU-27 (2019)[1]
- Road: 71,7 %
- Maritime: 14 %
- Air: 13,4 %
- Other: 0,5 %
- Railway: 0,4 %

Freight Transport in the EU (2021)[2]
- Maritime: 67,9 %
- Road: 24,6 %
- Rail: 5,4 %
- Inland waterways: 1,8 %
- Air: 0,2 %

Average cost of passenger traffic per person per kilometre (blue) and of freight traffic per tonne per kilometre (brown) in eurocents[3]
- Cars: 10,8
- Buses: 2,97
- Railway (passengers): 3,2
- Domestic flights: 12,77
- Railway (freight): 2,04
- Inland waterway vessels: 2,1
- HGV (heavy goods vehicles): 4,46
- Vans: 17,97

Data sources: [1] Europäische Umweltagentur, 2022, https://www.europarl.europa.eu/news/de/headlines/society/20190313STO31218/co2-emissionen-von-pkw-zahlen-und-fakten-infografik, [2] eurostat Statistics Explained, Eurostat, February 2023, https://ec.europa.eu/eurostat/statistics-explained/index.php?action=statexp-dc-display&title=Freight_transport_statistics_-_modal_split, [3] Heinrich-Böll-Stiftung/VCD Verkehrsclub Deutschland e.V.: Mobilitätsatlas 2019.

HOW TO USE

Passive Voice	
Anwendung:	
Aktiv: Verb im Aktiv drückt aus, was ein Subjekt macht.	Dinah **drives** the forklift. (Dinah fährt den Gabelstapler.)
Passiv: Verb im Passiv drückt aus, was mit dem Subjekt geschieht.	The forklift **is driven** by Dinah. (Der Gabelstapler wird von Dinah gefahren.)

Bildung:
Passive Voice = Form von „to be" + past participle („-ed" oder 3. Form des unregelmäßigen Verbs)

Zeit	Aktiv	Passiv
Simple Present	John packs parcels every day. (John packt jeden Tag Pakete.)	Parcels **are** pack**ed** by John every day. (Jeden Tag werden von John Pakete gepackt.)
Simple Past	John packed a parcel. (John packte ein Paket.)	A parcel **was** pack**ed** by John. (Ein Paket wurde von John gepackt.)
Present Continuous	John is packing a parcel. (John packt gerade ein Paket.)	A parcel **is being** pack**ed** by John. (Ein Paket wird gerade von John gepackt.)
Present Perfect	John has packed a parcel. (John hat ein Paket gepackt.)	A parcel **has been** pack**ed** by John. (Ein Paket wurde von John gepackt.)
Will-Future	John will pack a parcel. (John wird ein Paket packen.)	A parcel **will be** pack**ed** by John. (Ein Paket wird von John gepackt werden.)

Achtung:
– Bei der Umwandlung von Aktiv/Passiv darf die Zeit nicht gewechselt werden.

5.4.6 EXERCISE

Rewrite the sentences in the passive voice.

1. Eric drives a forklift truck every day.

2. Lucas has sent the consignment.

3. A new company cleaned our warehouse yesterday.

4. The sales representative will phone the customer immediately.

5.4.7 READING

Read the text and answer the questions below.

Multimodal Transport

1 Over the past decades the world has seen a movement towards globalisation and trade liberalisation. In this process, national borders are increasingly disappearing and trade barriers have been reduced or do not exist anymore. This development requires changes in the type and quality of transport and logistics services and infrastructure. The massive growth in containeri-
5 sation has shifted the modern transport from 'port-to-port' to 'door-to-door'. Moreover, many companies have changed their production methods to be able to use containers for export and to take advantage of Multimodal Transport (MT).

MT, also called combined transport, can be defined as the chain that links different modes of transport into one complete process. The intelligent combination of transport by air, by
10 road, by rail, or by sea ensures efficient and cost-effective door-to-door movement of goods. Multimodal transports are performed under the responsibility of a single transport operator, known as a Multimodal Transport Operator (MTO), on one transport document.

In today's dynamic markets companies must be flexible to respond rapidly to competition and market changes. The ultimate goal is to "deliver greater value to customers or create more
15 value at lower costs". Multimodal Transport is one option for companies to reduce costs and to improve customer service.

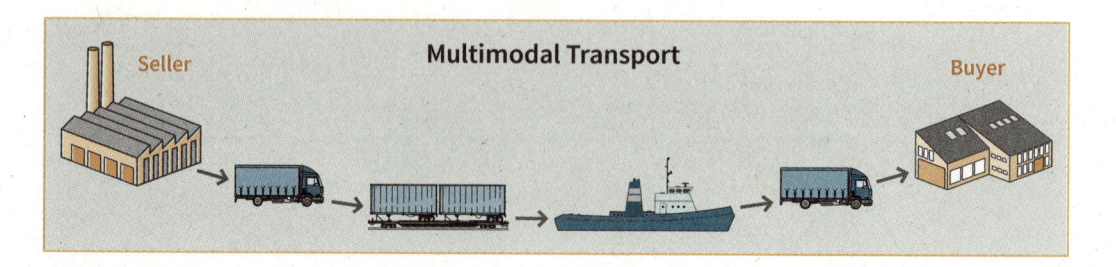

Transport and Logistics

5

1. What are the consequences of globalisation in general and for the logistics industry in particular?

2. What is a Multimodal Transport?

3. Which advantages of Multimodal Transport are mentioned in the text?

4. What challenges do companies face?

WORD BANK

containerisation	Container-Transport
corporate image	Firmenbild
decade	Jahrzehnt
to perform	auftreten, durchführen
revenue	Umsatz
to take advantage of	einen Vorteil aus etwas ziehen
trade barrier	Handelsschranke
transport operator	Transportunternehmer
ultimate goal	Endziel

5.5 Material Handling Equipment for Internal Transport

5.5.1 MATCHING

Nowadays, most work processes in a warehouse are based on high-tech equipment. The photos show different material handling equipment that can be used depending on the size, weight and nature of the goods. Match the names below to the photos and find the German equivalents.

autonomous mobile robot (AMR) | electric forklift truck | horizontal order picker | driver-seated reach truck | low-lift pallet truck | electric tractor | hand pallet truck | high-lift pallet truck

5.5.2 ANALYSING

a. Analyse the illustration below and mark the zones (1) – (6) on the storage plan.
b. In which zones is the material handling equipment pictured in 5.5.1 normally used?

c. Which other material handling equipment do you use in your daily work?

| (1) loading area with ramp | (3) shelf-storage system | (5) packing station |
| (2) receipt of goods | (4) order picking | (6) dispatch |

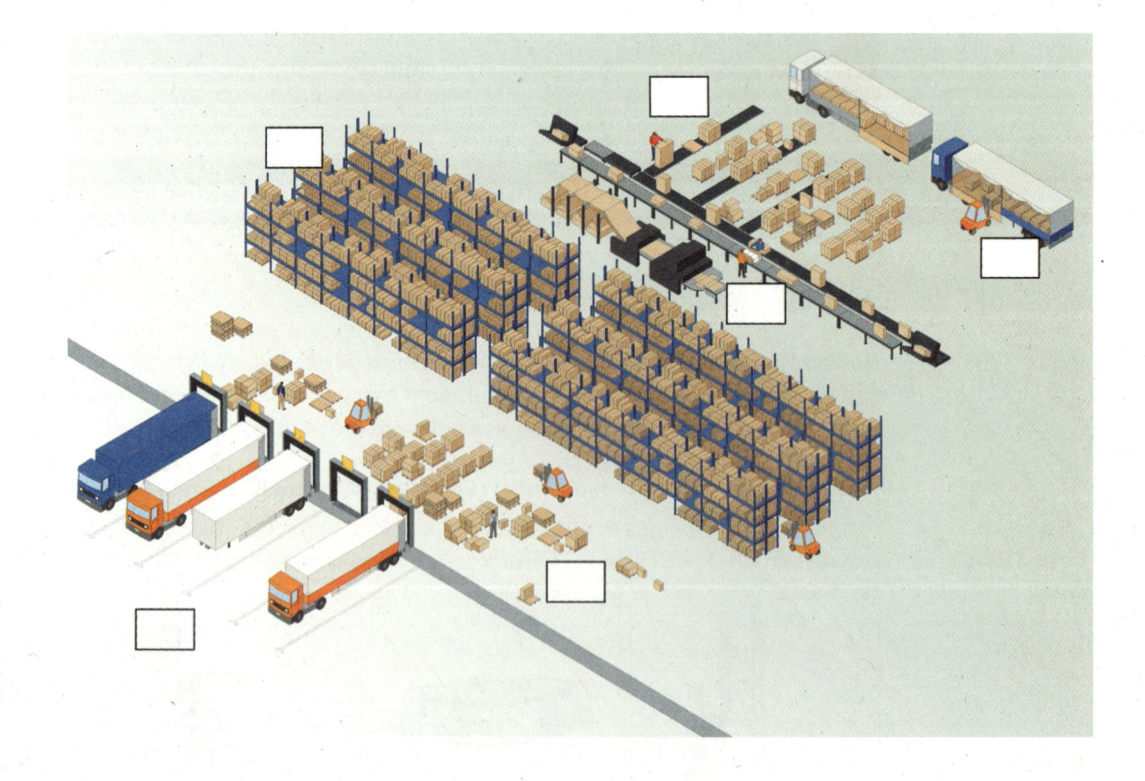

122

Transport and Logistics

5.5.3 CREATIVE ACTIVITY

Draw a storage plan of your stock room. Then explain the different zones and their functions in the whole process. Use the words from 5.5.2.

5.5.4 MATCHING

Forklift trucks have become the most important material handling vehicle in modern warehouses. They are extensively used in warehouses for loading and off-loading.

Look at the parts of a forklift truck. Use the words in the box to complete the drawing.

> counterbalance | driver's seat | engine compartment | fork | forklift fork | frame | lifting chain | lifting cylinder | mast | overhead guard | safety guard | tilt cylinders

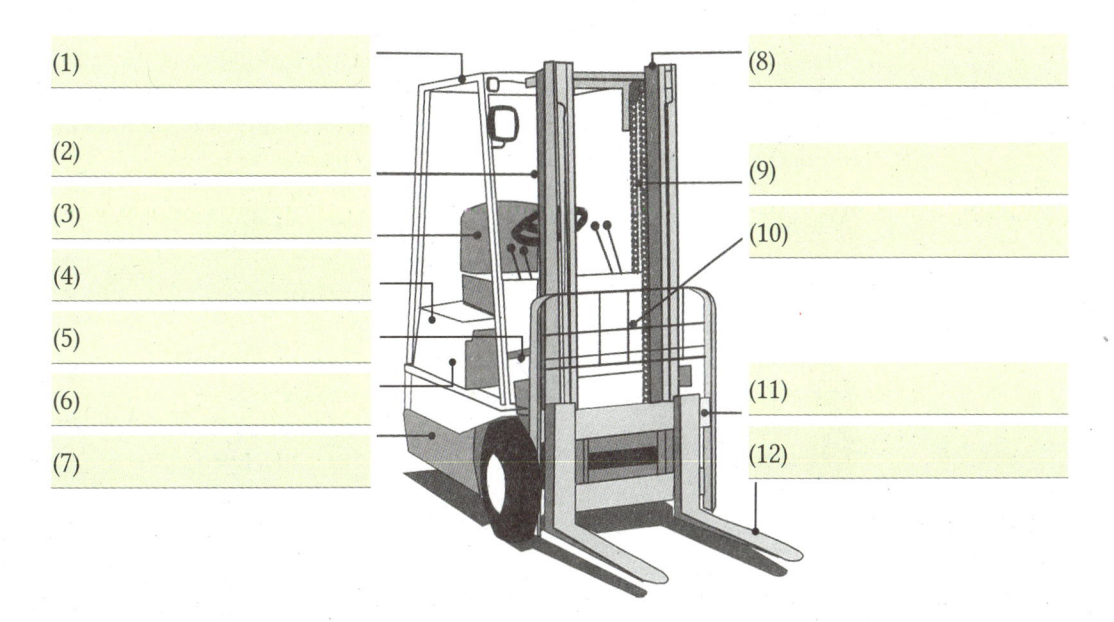

(1) _____
(2) _____
(3) _____
(4) _____
(5) _____
(6) _____
(7) _____
(8) _____
(9) _____
(10) _____
(11) _____
(12) _____

5 Transport and Logistics

5.6 Documents in National and International Trade

5.6.1 MATCHING

Goods can be shipped by the four modes of transport. The delivery can be performed by different means of transport. Different carriers require different shipping documents. Match the means of transport to the corresponding shipping documents.

1. freight forwarder by lorry
2. seller's lorry
3. courier, express and parcel services
4. cargo train
5. inland waterway vessel
6. seagoing vessel
7. transport plane

a. parcel label
b. bill of lading
c. air bill of lading
d. delivery note
e. consignment note/delivery note
f. railway bill of lading
g. bill of lading

5.6.2 READING

a. Read the text below carefully and fill in the commercial invoice on page 125. This is the invoice for the 200 pallet boxes, item no. 40-10202, you ordered with the form on page 102.

Delivery Notes

1 A delivery note is a document that **accompanies** a shipment of goods. It includes information about quantity, description, **grade**, weight and the delivery date of the goods delivered. The delivery note is issued by the supplier and a copy of the delivery note, signed by the buyer, is returned to the seller. It **serves** as **proof** that the goods have been delivered. On delivery the
5 buyer needs to check the note carefully. In case of damage the delivery can be **rejected**.

The **commercial invoice** sometimes serving as a delivery note is also issued by the supplier. In addition to the listed information, a commercial invoice also includes elements such as name and address of seller and buyer, the invoice number, unit price and total price, shipping details (number of packages) or terms of delivery and payment.

WORD BANK	
to accompany	begleiten, beifügen
bill of lading	Frachtbrief
commercial invoice	Warenrechnung
freight forwarder	Spediteur
grade	Grad, Anspruchsklasse
parcel label	Paketaufkleber
proof	Beweis, Abzug
to reject	abweisen, ablehnen
seagoing vessel	Seeschiff
to serve	dienen, nützen

Transport and Logistics

b. Discuss with your partner which difficulties might appear in filling in and checking delivery notes.

GT Global Transport Ltd.

Commercial invoice

Exporter/Shipper (name and adress)	Invoice number
Consignee	Invoice date
	Manufacturing country
Terms of payment	Destination country
Freight	Other remarks

Item	Weight	Description of goods	Quantity	Unit price	Amount
Total weight			Total quantity	Total invoice amount	

Name of Shipper

Signature of Shipper

5 Transport and Logistics

5.7 Innovations in Warehousing and Logistics

5.7.1 READING

1 "If I had asked the public what they wanted, they would have said a faster horse." This quote by Henry Ford, founder of Ford Motor Company, says a lot about inventors and their ambition to change things for the better. Companies who have been around for many years do the same. They try to remain state of the art or even set new standards with innovative products.
5 Identifying trends and understanding the customer's needs are fundamental for successful businesses.

The same applies to warehousing and logistics. It has always been an extremely dynamic and fast-growing industry. New technologies have emerged and are having an enormous impact on how goods are stored and carried. Manual work has become less important; analogue me-
10 dia has been replaced by digital tools, such as scanners, RFID-technology or cloud computing technology.

But what options do companies that are operating in such a dynamic market really have? On the one hand, businesses can adapt to new developments and implement modern technologies, but that is costly and requires much know-how. On the other hand, they could just leave things
15 as they are. Small and medium-sized companies especially often do not have the financial means to invest a crazy amount of money.

Howsoever, things are changing all the time and new technologies are changing the way we do business and work. If professionals 40 years ago had heard of a fully automated warehouse, driverless transport systems or even robots, they would not have believed it. For young pro-
20 fessionals starting a career in this industry, it is a balancing act between enthusiasm for new technologies and their concerns about their role in the warehouse of the future.

Read the text below carefully and answer the following questions.

1. What should companies do to be successful in the market?

2. Name trends in the warehousing and logistics industry.

3. Which options do businesses have to face the changes?

4. Name innovations based on automatisation or digitalisation.

Transport and Logistics

5.7.2 WRITING

Discuss Henry Ford's quote *"If I had asked the public what they wanted, they would have said a faster horse."*

5.7.3 MATCHING

Read the articles on innovations in the warehousing and logistics industry. Then match the headlines with the articles.

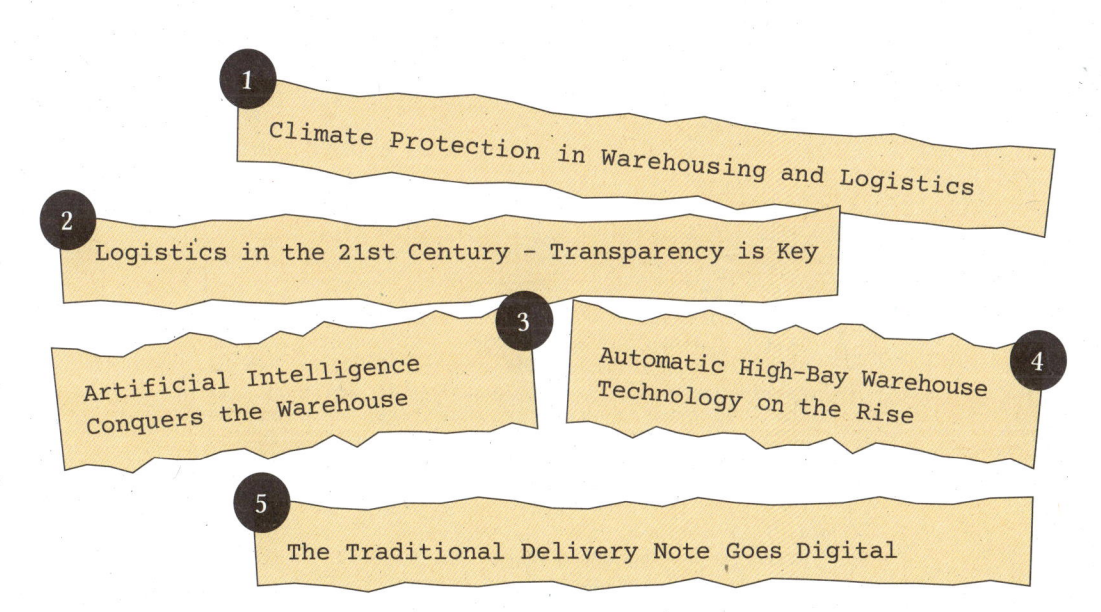

1. Climate Protection in Warehousing and Logistics
2. Logistics in the 21st Century – Transparency is Key
3. Artificial Intelligence Conquers the Warehouse
4. Automatic High-Bay Warehouse Technology on the Rise
5. The Traditional Delivery Note Goes Digital

Tracking & Tracing is also referred to as shipment tracking. Usually accurate digital documentation and tracking of a shipment from start at the shipper to delivery to the recipient. End consumers are familiar with this from the tracking of postal shipments. In the shipping operations of freight forwarding and logistics, tracking & tracing is also used. Shipments can be located at any time and entire shipping processes can be tracked. Tracking describes the determination of the current status and tracing means the traceability of the exact course of the shipment.

Source: LIS Logistics Informations System GmbH: Tracking & Tracing, in: https://www.lis.eu/en/lexikon/tracking-tracing-draft/ [04.04.2023]

Traditional warehousing lends thought to factors like shipping schedules, storage space, and packaging materials. Anything that keeps orders moving through the center on time is acceptable. Green warehousing is the idea that fulfillment centers can do more than create environmental pollution. With specific strategies, any warehouse can reduce its carbon footprint.

Source: Morrison, Rose: What Is Green Warehousing? (And How to Achieve It), in: Unsustainable, 16.02.2022, www.unsustainablemagazine.com/what-is-green-warehousing/ [07.11.2022]

Transport and Logistics

Technological advancements and an increasingly competitive business landscape are forcing modern warehouses to seriously consider the use of robotics. With their ability to increase productivity, accuracy and operational efficiency, warehouse robots are no longer nice-to-have accessories – they have become indispensable to efficient warehouse operations. Warehouse automations of all kinds add value to warehousing operations by automating the execution of menial, repetitive tasks, thus allowing human workers to focus on more complicated tasks.

Source: 6 River Systems: What is warehouse robotics?, 25.08.2022, https://6river.com/what-is-warehouse-robotics/.

If goods have to be stored densely in a small area, a customised high-bay warehouse system with fully automated storage and retrieval from goods receipt to dispatch is recommended. It is suitable for pallets, boxes, rolls, stacks, trays or cardboard boxes in different formats and with different weights. High-bay warehouses for very large throughput and a wide variety of articles can be built for single-deep or double-deep storage. [...] Channel storage systems with multi-deep storage and the highest degree of automation are a particularly space-saving and efficient solution for warehouses with larger stocks per article.

Source: HÖRMANN Intralogistics GmbH: Automated high-bay warehouses - individual and highly available, o. ED., https://www.hoermann-intralogistics.com/en/intralogistics/automatic-high-bay-warehouse. [04.04.2023]

The shipper on the supplier side stores the delivery notes in the cloud. GS1 identification standards ensure that the digital document can be assigned clearly to the particular delivery. If the logistics service provider takes care of the load, the driver scans a QR code generated in the manufacturer's outgoing goods department. All that is needed is a smartphone with a scanning function (via the integrated camera). The link to the digital delivery note is stored as a card in the driver's smartphone wallet - a function which is already used for airline or concert tickets.
During transport, the digital delivery note documents can be retrieved at any time and can be presented during inspections. At the retailer's incoming goods department, the digital delivery note is read in again from the cloud for further processing by scanning the QR code on the driver's smartphone and can be signed off here.

Source: Messe München GmbH: Digital trade documents, in: drinktec Blog, 10.08.2022, https://blog.drinktec.com/cross-industry/digital-trade-documents/ [07.11.2022]

5.7.4 ANALYSIS

Based on our recent findings, let us take a critical look at the consequences of innovations and modern technology in warehousing and logistics.

Use the method "Think-Pair-Share" for completing the table on the next page.

> **Method "Think-Pair-Share"**
> Think: In this phase you think individually about a specific question. Feel free to take notes or structure your ideas by using a mindmap. This part can take up to ten minutes.
> Pair: For this part, you pair up. You share with another classmate everything you have come up with. You can be given at least five minutes for this part of the activity.
> Share: The results of your pair work are now shared with the class.

Modern technology in warehousing and logistics – Threat or Opportunity?		
	Employee's perspective	Employer's perspective
Benefits		
Drawbacks		

5.7.5 CREATIVE WRITING

Write a text about what the warehouse of the future will look like. Let your creativity flow.

5.7.6 PROJECT BASED LEARNING

Warehousing and Logistics in the 21st Century

I. Introduction
Nothing lasts forever. This saying is especially true for the business world in the 21st century. Nowadays, companies are facing permanent changes and competition has become a global challenge, which needs smart answers in order to be successful on the global market.

Through the project you will learn why challenges like "Digitalisation" and the "Shortage of skilled workers" are of paramount importance for companies doing business in warehousing and in the logistics industry.

Therefore, our learning tool Project Based Learning (PBL) centres on aspects modern companies should implement in their corporate identity as well as into daily operations.

II. Objectives
After this project you will have learnt about:
- Innovations and technologies that are already found in the warehouses of today
- Innovative approaches and technologies for the design of the warehouse of the future.
- The impact of high-tech technologies like artificial intelligence on warehouse operations.
- The importance of leadership and strategies to cope with the shortage of skilled workers.
- The importance of a highly skilled and highly motivated workforce, and a range of incentives given by companies to keep the current workforce motivated and to attract a skilled workforce.

Transport and Logistics

III. Process and Task

a. Team up and decide which of the objectives below you would like to deal with.

Project Theme	Key words	Teammates
1. The warehouse of the future	technology, digitisation, automatisation, artificial intelligence, digital delivery note	
2. Benefits and drawbacks of an automated warehouse	pros and cons from the company's and the worker's perspective	
3. If I were the warehouse manager, I would change …	face-to-face contact, working atmosphere, internal workflow, use of technology	
4. Corporate incentives and strategies to increase employee satisfaction and to attract new workers	incentives, leadership (style), employee satisfaction, skills shortage	

b. Once you have chosen the project theme and it has been confirmed by the audience, start planning your project (aspects given by the teacher, division of labour within the group, types of media you want to use, set deadlines, etc.).

c. Based on the stated objectives, plan, discuss and submit your agenda for your presentation to the teacher as soon as possible to avoid "being on the wrong track".

d. Prepare a presentation that meets the standards of how presentations are delivered by the speaker and what a digital presentation (PowerPoint presentation, Prezi, etc.) should look like.

SKILLS

Project Based Learning (PBL)

Project Based Learning is a team-based learning method with regular team check-ins and meetings with the teacher. Once the PBL has been launched and core content and concept presented by the teacher and discussed by the audience, students gather, share and evaluate information on a specific topic.

In the course of a PBL, students improve their teambuilding and communicative skills as well as language skills. Moreover, creating a product and presenting the results to an audience has positive effects on self-esteem and personal development.

Transport and Logistics

5.8 Business Correspondence – Complaints and Apologies

5.8.1 BRAINSTORMING

Read the text and with a partner brainstorm reasons for a complaint. Make a mind map from your results.

Sometimes Things Go Wrong

1. When selling products or services, mistakes sometimes happen. In this case the customer will complain to the supplier. Dealing with customer complaints is one of the most delicate issues in business as the aim is to satisfy and retain the customer. You should therefore respond to a complaint in a polite tone. Give the customer the feeling that you understand his/her problem
5. and that you will solve the problem. The customer also expects you to take action either in granting compensation or, if the complaint is not fully justified, in suggesting a compromise. It should in any case meet the customer's expectations.

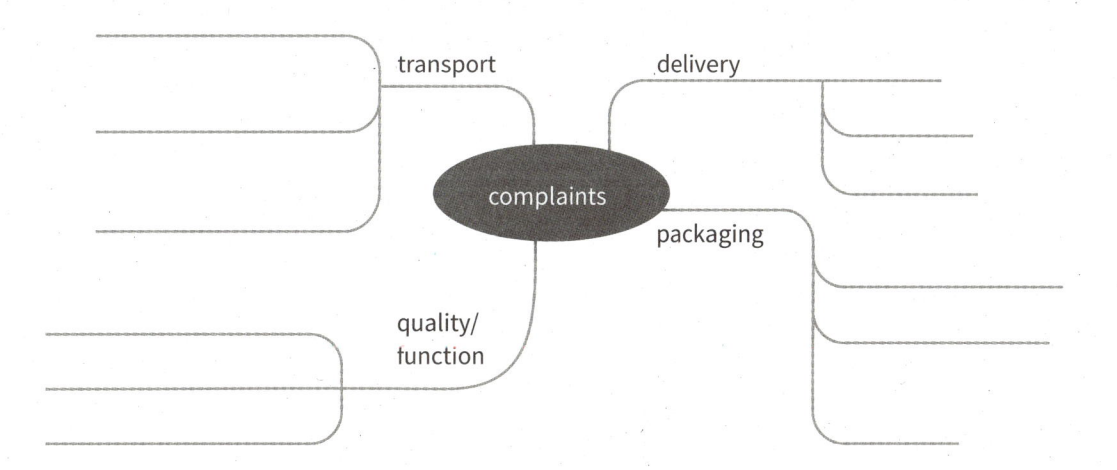

Mind map with central node "complaints" and branches: transport, delivery, packaging, quality/function.

5.8.2 READING

Read the letter of complaint on page 132 and decide if the statements below are true or false.

TRUE (=T) OR FALSE (=F)

1. *Fragrance Makers* received a consignment of bottles and jars.
2. 24 bottles are broken and 3 jars are missing.
3. They are sending photos of the bottles and jars to prove the damage.
4. The damage was caused by rough handling in transit.
5. *Fragrance Makers* do not need the replacement before next month.
6. The damaged items will be returned to the supplier.

Transport and Logistics

From: bruce.haven@fragrancemakers.com
To: lex.cole@fancybottles.co.uk
Date: 10 October 20...
Subject: Damaged items

Dear Mr Cole

Our order no. 1234
Your packing list no. 6543

We are writing with reference to the above mentioned consignment of perfume bottles and jars we received yesterday.

On unpacking the items we found that 9 of the 24 bottles in parcel no. 5 were completely broken and 3 of the 30 jars in parcel no. 6 were badly scratched.

We are attaching photographs of the damaged items as evidence for our complaint.
As you can see from the photos, the damage was obviously caused by faulty packing and insufficient labelling. The parcels had neither a label nor a handling sign indicating "fragile". Moreover, the padding in these particular parcels was almost completely missing.

As bottling of the perfume is scheduled for next week, please arrange the immediate shipment of the replacement at your expense.

Regarding the faulty articles, we are keeping them in our warehouse awaiting your instructions.

We look forward to your early reply.

Yours sincerely
Bruce Haven
Purchasing Manager

FragranceMakers
102-104 Barlow Road * Cheshire, CW7 2RB
Phone: 0044(0)1606-874589 * Fax: 0044(0)1606-874590

WORD BANK

apology	Entschuldigung
breakage	Bruch
complaint	Beschwerde
evidence	Beweis
faulty	fehlerhaft
insufficient	unzureichend
imprint	Eindruck
jar	Glas(gefäß)
padding	Auspolsterung, Füllmaterial
replacement	Ersatz
scratched	verkratzt

Transport and Logistics

5.8.3 LISTENING FOR GIST

Listen to the telephone conversation and make notes.

What is Mr Brandt's problem?	What does Ms Wise find out?	How does Ms Wise solve the problem?

5.8.4. LISTENING FOR DETAIL

Listen to the conversation again and complete the sentences with the expressions from the box.

> my records | place of destination | regret | at the latest | highly important | accept our apologies | rely on | delivery note | before | DE-76934 | express delivery | see to it | misaddressed | key it in

1. Could you please give me the number of the (1) _____?

2. Just a moment, I have to check (2) _____. Okay, here we are, the delivery note number is (3) _____.

3. I have to (4) _____ to get the details of the delivery.

4. The first consignment went to the correct address while the second one was (5) _____.

5. Actually, we need them immediately, Ms Wise, by Friday (6) _____ as I have promised them to one of our (7) _____ customers.

6. Okay, I'll (8) _____ that another consignment is sent to your correct address by (9) _____. Usually, it takes one to two days to arrive at the (10) _____.

7. I think you should receive the goods (11) _____ Friday.

8. I (12) _____ having caused you such trouble.

9. I'll (13) _____ you and expect the delivery before Friday, then.

10. Certainly, Mr Brandt, and once again, please (14) _____ for this mistake.

133

5.8.5 MATCHING

How to structure a reply to a customer's complaint
1. Refer to the complaint and thank them for the feedback.
2. Apologise for the problem and express understanding.
3. Explain the problem.
4. Make a suggestion to solve the problem.(Compensation)
5. Apologise again; assure them this will not happen again.
6. Close the letter.

- [ ] I am sorry to hear that your parcel has not arrived.
- [ ] Once again, I apologise for the inconvenience.
- [ ] We are sorry for the inconvenience you had with our service.
- [ ] As compensation, we can offer you a price reduction of 25 %.
- [ ] We have already arranged for a replacement of the faulty goods.
- [ ] First, I would like to apologise for the problem you have experienced.
- [ ] We assure you that we will do everything to improve our service.
- [ ] We are looking forward to doing further business with you.
- [ ] We have checked the matter and found out that there was a problem with the filling machine.

5.8.6 WRITING

Translate into English.

1. Vielen Dank für Ihren Anruf vom 14. Juni 20..

2. Wir entschuldigen uns für die fehlerhaften Artikel.

3. Wir haben bereits eine Expresslieferung von Ersatzartikeln veranlasst.

4. Wir haben die Angelegenheit überprüft und festgestellt, dass es ein technisches Problem bei der Fertigungsanlage gab.

5. Als Ausgleich für die Unannehmlichkeiten haben wir bereits eine Preisreduzierung um 25 % veranlasst.

Transport and Logistics

6. Wir tun alles, um unseren Service zu verbessern.

5.8.7 WRITING

You work for *Canny Ltd.*, a producer of canned food, located in 127 Highhill Road, Glasgow G2 7 DL. Your boss has asked you to write a reply to a complaint to Mr Gordon Splash of *Golden Knife*, a catering company. The address of *Golden Knife* is 87 Victoria Road, Dundee DD1 4DU.

Use these notes and the following sample of a reply to a complaint to compose your letter:

- refer to order No. GS-459
- thank him for the message of 18 October and the information that the canned tomatoes have not been delivered yet
- you found out that the delay is due to a defect of the can closing machine
- you have arranged for immediate delivery
- to make up for the inconvenience you include a sample of premium class tomato soup
- apologise for the inconvenience caused
- close the letter

Example of a reply to a complaint

The Textile Company   308 Morgan Street, London WIA 3B2
Phone 071 288 5689 Fax 071 288 5680

www.textile.company.co.uk

4 September 20..

Ms Judith Sorento
Bellevue Hotel
144 Seaside Road
Brighton
BN 1 1NS

Dear Ms Sorento

Order No St-9015

Thank you for your message of 3 September 20.. in which you informed us about the wrong content of parcel No. 9 of the consignment we sent to you last week.

We have checked the matter and found out that in fact this parcel was originally intended to go to a different customer and therefore contained cutlery instead of sun shades.

I have already arranged for express delivery of the correct articles, which should reach you tomorrow. As a small compensation for the mistake, we have included 3 tablecloths which go very well with the ordered sun shades.

Would you please be so kind and return the cutlery to our warehouse. We will refund the carriage costs to your account.

Please accept our apology for the inconvenience.

We look forward to doing further business with you.

Yours sincerely
Nigel Fox
Sales Department

5 Transport and Logistics

5.8.8 CROSSWORD

Complete the crossword.

ACROSS
1. Umsatz
3. zerbrechlich
4. verschicken
7. Wettbewerb
10. Beschwerde
11. zuverlässig
12. Palette

DOWN
2. Umwelt
5. Rechnung
6. Kunde
8. Zulieferer
9. Lieferung

Phonetic Alphabet

Für die englische Lautschrift wurden die phonetischen Zeichen des IPA (International Phonetic Alphabet) verwendet.

Vokale und Diphtonge		Konsonanten	
ɪ	sit	p	pen
e	best	b	bus
æ	cat	t	time
ɒ[BE]	pot	d	do
ʌ	much	k	cat
ʊ	book	g	girl
ə	about	f	fall
i	happy	v	very
u	annual	θ	think
iː	see	ð	this
ɑː	card	s	soft
ɔː	saw	z	zoo
uː	too	ʃ	show
ɜː	bird	ʒ	vision
eɪ	date	h	hot
aɪ	my	tʃ	chip
ɔɪ	boy	dʒ	juice
əʊ[BE]	go	m	man
aʊ	house	n	not
ʊə[BE]	sure	ŋ	ring
eə[BE]	hair	l	let
ɪə[BE]	real	w	why
		r	right
		j	yes

Die dargestellte Lautschrift gibt grundsätzlich die britische Aussprache wieder. Die in Klammern stehenden Lautsymbole (ə) und (r) werden, abhängig vom englischen Sprachraum, ausgesprochen oder nicht. Im amerikanischen Englisch wird (r) üblicherweise mit ausgesprochen. In der Lautschrift werden zwei Betonungszeichen benutzt, die kennzeichnen, welche Silbe bzw. welcher Wortteil betont werden muss. ˈ bestimmt den Hauptton, ˌ den schwächeren Ton.

Word Banks

UNIT 1

WORD BANK 1

apprenticeship	[əˈprentɪʃɪp]	Ausbildungsplatz
employee	[ˌemplɔɪˈi]	Mitarbeiter/-in
goods issue	[gʊdz ˈɪʃjuː]	Warenausgang
goods receipt	[gʊdz rɪˈsiːt]	Wareneingang
location	[ləʊˈkeɪʃn]	Standort
stock	[stɒk]	Lager
warehouse administration	[ˈweəhaʊz ədˌmɪnɪˈstreɪʃn]	Lagerverwaltung
warehouse operator	[ˈweəhaʊz ˈɒpəreɪtə]	Fachlagerist/-in
warehouse supervisor	[ˈweəhaʊz ˈsuːpəvaɪzə]	Lagerleiter/-in
workplace	[ˈwɜːkpleɪs]	Arbeitsplatz

WORD BANK 2

customised	[ˈkʌstəmaɪzd]	kundenspezifisch
dedicated	[ˈdedɪkeɪtɪd]	engagiert
groceries	[ˈgrəʊsərɪz]	Lebensmittel
organic food	[ɔːˈgænɪk fuːd]	Biolebensmittel
to provide with	[prəˈvaɪd wɪð]	versorgen mit
to purchase	[pɜːtʃəs]	(ein)kaufen
resource	[rɪˈsɔːs]	Mittel
retail	[riːˈteɪl]	Einzelhandel
staff	[staːf]	Belegschaft, Mitarbeiter
success	[səkˈses]	Erfolg
support	[səˈpɔːt]	Unterstützung
wholesaler	[ˈhəʊlˌseɪlə]	Großhändler

WORD BANK 3

to accelerate	[əkˈseləreɪt]	zunehmen
founder	[ˈfaʊndə]	Gründer/-in
considerable	[kənˈsɪd(ə)rəb(ə)l]	beträchtlich, beachtlich
to establish	[ɪˈstæblɪʃ]	errichten, gründen
to expand	[ɪkˈspænd]	expandieren, erweitern
factory	[ˈfæktri]	Fabrik
to flourish	[ˈflʌrɪʃ]	florieren
growth	[grəʊθ]	Wachstum
humble	[ˈhʌmb(ə)l]	bescheiden
in turn	[ɪn ˈtɜː(r)n]	wiederum
to inaugurate	[ɪˈnɔːgjʊreɪt]	einweihen
owner	[ˈəʊnə]	Eigentümer/-in
product line	[ˈprɒdʌkt laɪn]	Sortiment
relocation	[riːləʊˈkeɪʃn]	Umzug/Verlegung
shortage	[ˈʃɔː(r)tɪdʒ]	Engpass
to take over	[teɪk ˈəʊvə(r)]	übernehmen

Word Banks

WORD BANK 4

to arrange	[əˈreɪndʒ]	ausmachen, arrangieren
to be tied up	[bi: taɪd ʌp]	beschäftigt sein
briefing	[briːfɪŋ]	Einsatzbesprechung
demanding	[dɪˈmɑːndɪŋ]	fordernd
engineer	[ˌendʒɪˈbɪə]	Techniker/-in
to look forward to doing sth.	[lʊk ˈfɔːwəd tuː]	sich darauf freuen, etwas zu tun
to manage sth.	[ˈmænɪdʒ]	es schaffen, etwas zu tun
schedule	[ˈskedjuːl]	Zeitplan
smoothly	[smuːðlɪ]	glatt, ohne Probleme
to suggest	[səˈdʒest]	vorschlagen
vacancy	[ˈveɪkənsɪ]	offene Arbeitsstelle

WORD BANK 5

(…)	in brackets	[ɪn ˈbrækɪts]	in Klammern
(	open bracket	[ˈəʊpən ˈbrækɪt]	Klammer auf
)	close bracket	[kləʊz ˈbrækɪt]	Klammer zu
/	slash	[slæʃ]	Schrägstrich
–	dash	[dæʃ]	Gedankenstrich
_	underscore	[ˌʌndə(r)ˈskɔː(r)]	Unterstrich
@	at	[æt]	at
.	dot (in e-mails)	[dɒt]	Punkt

UNIT 2

WORD BANK 1

ankle	[ˈæŋkl]	Fußgelenk, Fußknöchel
to become familiar with sth.	[bɪˈkʌm fəˈnɪljə wɪð]	mit etwas vertraut werden
bruise	[bruːz]	Prellung, Bluterguss
compensation	[ˌkɒmpenˈseɪʃn]	Schmerzensgeld, Schadensersatz
concrete floor	[kənˈkriːt flɔː]	Betonboden
to crush	[krʌʃ]	quetschen, zerdrücken
fatality	[fəˈtælətɪ]	Unglück, Todesfall
fireproof	[ˈfaɪəpruːf]	feuerfest, feuerbeständig
hazard	[ˈhæzəd]	Gefahr, Risiko
injury	[ˈɪndʒərɪ]	Verwundung, Verletzung
to kneel down	[niːl daʊn]	sich hinknien
measure	[ˌmeʒə]	Maßnahme
to occur	[əˈkɜː]	auftreten
precautions	[prɪˈkɔːʃnz]	Vorsichtsmaßnahmen
to prohibit	[prəˈhɪbɪt]	verbieten
severe	[sɪˈvɪə]	ernst, schlimm, schwer
slips and trips	[slɪps ænd trɪps]	Ausrutschen und Stolpern
theft	[θeft]	Diebstahl
threat	[θret]	Drohung, Gefährdung

Word Banks

WORD BANK 2

ample	[ˈæmpl]	geräumig, ausgiebig
to avoid	[əˈvɔɪd]	verhindern
to bump into sth./so.	[bʌmp ˈɪntʊ]	mit etwas/jemandem zusammenstoßen
common	[ˈkɒmən]	alltäglich, häufig, bekannt
entire	[ɪnˈtaɪə]	ganz, komplett
to exceed	[ɪkˈsiːd]	übertreffen
inspection	[ɪnˈspekʃən]	Prüfung, Kontrolle
manual handling	[ˈmænjʊəl ˈhændlɪŋ]	manuelle Handhabung
novice	[ˈnɒvɪs]	Anfänger/-in, Neuling
odd	[ɒd]	seltsam
to pinpoint	[ˈpɪnpɔɪnt]	genau bestimmen, festlegen
posture	[ˈpɒstʃə]	Haltung, Körperhaltung

WORD BANK 3

delivery date	[dɪˈlɪvəri deɪt]	Liefertermin
discount	[ˈdɪskaʊnt]	Rabatt, Ermäßigung
to grant	[grɑːnt]	gewähren, einräumen
grateful	[ˈgreɪtfʊl]	dankbar
range of	[reɪndʒ əv]	Auswahl/Angebot an
to rephrase	[rɪˈfreɪz]	umformulieren
requirement	[rɪˈkwaɪəmənt]	Anforderung
substantial	[səbˈstænʃl]	umfangreich, beträchtlich
terms of delivery	[tɜːmz əv dɪˈlɪvəri]	Lieferbedingungen
terms of payment	[tɜːmz əv ˈpeɪmənt]	Zahlungsbedingungen

UNIT 3

WORD BANK 1

apparently	[əˈpærəntli]	anscheinend, augenscheinlich
to check	[tʃæk]	prüfen
condition	[kənˈdɪʃn]	Zustand
delivery note	[dɪˈlɪvəri nəʊt]	Lieferschein
to document	[ˈdɒkjʊmənt]	beurkunden, dokumentieren
to exchange sth.	[ɪksˈtʃeɪndʒ]	etwas austauschen
offer	[ˈɒfə]	Angebot
order	[ˈɔːdə]	Auftrag
purchasing department	[ˈpɜːtʃəsɪŋ dɪˈpɑːtmənt]	Einkaufsabteilung
reusable	[ˌriːˈjuːsəbl]	wieder verwendbar, Mehrweg-
to sign a receipt	[saɪn ə rɪˈsiːt]	eine Quittung unterschreiben
stock list	[ˈstɒk lɪst]	Lagerliste
to unload sth.	[ˌʌnˈləʊd]	etwas abladen

Word Banks

WORD BANK 2

accounting	[əˈkaʊntɪŋ]	Buchhaltung
air waybill	[ˈeə weɪbɪl]	Luftfrachtbrief
carrier	[ˈkærɪə]	Frachtführer
to complain about	[kəmˈpleɪn əˈbaʊt]	reklamieren, sich über etwas beschweren
consignment/delivery/shipment	[kənˈsaɪnmənt/dɪˈlɪvərɪ/ˈʃɪpmənt]	Lieferung
to correspond to	[ˌkɒrɪˈspɒnd tuː]	etwas entsprechen
forwarding documents	[ˈfɔːwədɪŋ ˈdɒkjʊmənts]	Warenbegleitpapiere
goods receipt slip	[gʊdz rɪˈsiːt slɪp]	Wareneingangsschein
invoice	[ˈɪnvɔɪs]	Rechnung
interface	[ˌɪntəˈfeɪs]	Schnittstelle
in stock	[ɪn stɒk]	auf Lager, vorrätig
packing list	[ˈpækɪŋ lɪst]	Packliste
quality control	[ˈkwɒlətɪ kənˈtrəʊl]	Qualitätskontrolle

WORD BANK 3

appropriate	[əˈprəʊprɪeɪt]	angemessen
by heart	[baɪ hɑːt]	auswendig
to consider	[kənˈsɪdə]	in Erwägung ziehen, betrachten
favourable	[ˈfeɪvərəbl]	günstig
to gain	[geɪn]	erlangen, aneignen
to follow rules/instructions	[ˈfɒləʊ ruːlz/ɪnˈstrʌkʃənz]	Regeln/Anweisungen befolgen
to omit	[əˈmɪt]	weglassen
to protect from	[prəˈtekt frɒm]	schützen vor
vermin	[ˈvɜːmɪn]	Schädlinge

WORD BANK 4

as a result	[əz ə rɪˈzʌlt]	schlussfolgernd
first of all	[fɜːst əv ɔːl]	zuerst, zuallererst
furthermore	[ˌfɜːðəˈmɔː]	außerdem, darüber hinaus
in addition	[ɪn əˈdɪʃn]	ergänzend, hinzu kommt
in my opinion	[ɪn maɪ əˈpɪnjən]	meiner Meinung nach
last but not least	[lɑːst bʌt nɒt liːst]	nicht zuletzt
on the one hand, on the other hand	[ɒn ðə wʌn hænd, ɒn ðiː ˈʌðə hænd]	auf der einen Seite, auf der anderen Seite
therefore	[ˈðeəfɔː]	somit, deshalb
to sum it up	[tuː sʌm ɪt ʌp]	um es zusammenzufassen
whereas	[weərˈæz]	wobei, wohingegen
while	[waɪl]	während

WORD BANK 5

advice	[ədˈvaɪs]	Rat, Empfehlung
competitive	[kəmˈpetətɪv]	wettbewerbsfähig

Word Banks

delivery time	[dɪˈlɪvəri ˈtaɪm]	Lieferzeitpunkt, Lieferfrist
enquiry	[ɪnˈkwaɪəri]	Anfrage
filing cabinet	[ˈfaɪlɪŋ ˈkæbɪnɪt]	Aktenschrank
located	[ləʊˈkeɪtɪd]	ansässig
luggage	[ˈlʌɡɪdʒ]	Gepäck
medium-sized	[ˈmiːdjəm saɪzd]	mittelständisch
pallet	[ˈpælɪt]	Palette
to redecorate	[riːˈdekəreɪt]	renovieren

UNIT 4

WORD BANK 1

to become redundant	[bɪˈkʌm rɪˈdʌndənt]	seinen Arbeitsplatz verlieren
to decrease	[ˈdiːkriːs]	fallen
(electronic) order picking	[ˌɪlekˈtrɒnɪk ˈɔːdə ˈpɪkɪŋ]	(beleglose) Kommissionierung
to facilitate	[fəˈsɪlɪteɪt]	erleichtern
to increase	[ɪnˈkriːs]	steigen
logistics	[ləˈdʒɪstɪks]	Versorgung, Logistik
low level order picking	[ləʊ ˌlevl ˈɔːdə ˈpɪkɪŋ]	maschinengestützte Kommissionierung
pick-by-barcode	[pɪk baɪ bɑːkəʊd]	Kommissionieren per Strichcode
pick-by-light	[pɪk baɪ laɪt]	Kommissionieren per LED-Anzeigen
pick-by-vision	[pɪk baɪ ˈvɪʒn]	Kommissionieren per Datenbrille
pick-by-voice	[pɪk baɪ vɔɪs]	Kommissionieren per Sprachbefehl
order picking by pick list	[ˈɔːdə ˈpɪkɪŋ baɪ pɪk lɪst]	beleghafte Kommissionierung
time-consuming	[taɪm kənˈsjuːmɪŋ]	zeitaufwändig

WORD BANK 2

cold storage	[kəʊld ˈstɔːrɪdʒ]	Kühllager
counterintuitive	[ˌkaʊnt(ə)rɪnˈtjuːɪtɪv]	widersinnig
fire hazard	[ˈfaɪə(r) ˈhæzə(r)d]	Brandgefahr
feasibility	[ˌfiːzəˈbɪləti]	Machbarkeit
refrigerated freight	[rɪˈfrɪdʒəreɪtɪd freɪt]	Kühltransport
demand	[dɪˈmɑːnd]	Nachfrage
fire safety	[ˈfaɪə(r) ˈseɪfti]	Brandschutz
safety equipment	[ˈseɪfti ɪˈkwɪpmənt]	Sicherheitsausrüstung
safety regulations	[ˈseɪfti ˌreɡjʊˈleɪʃ(ə)nz]	Sicherheitsvorschriften
to prevent	[prɪˈvent]	vermeiden
warehouse industry	[ˈweəhaʊz ˈɪndəstri]	Lagerbranche
economy	[ɪˈkɒnəmi]	Wirtschaft
billion	[ˈbɪljən]	Milliarde

Word Banks

WORD BANK 3

to provide	[prəˈvaɪd]	bereitstellen, anbieten
freight forwarding industry	[freɪt ˈfɔːwədɪŋ ˈɪndəstri]	Speditionsbranche
to reduce	[rɪˈdjuːs]	verringern
drive technology	[draɪv tekˈnɒlədʒi]	Antriebstechnologie
hydrogen	[ˈhaɪdrədʒən]	Wasserstoff
decarbonisation	[diːˌkɑ(r)bəniːseɪʃn]	Reduzierung von CO_2-Emissionen
to accelerate	[əkˈseləreɪt]	beschleunigen
to intend	[ɪnˈtend]	beabsichtigen, anstreben
steering	[ˈstɪərɪŋ]	Lenkung, Steuerung
additional	[əˈdɪʃ(ə)nəl]	zusätzlich
average	[ˈæv(ə)rɪdʒ]	Durchschnitt
apprenticeship	[əˈprentɪsʃɪp]	Ausbildung
curriculum vitae	[kəˌrɪkjʊləm ˈviːtaɪ]	Lebenslauf

WORD BANK 4

confirmation	[ˌkɑnfəˈmeɪʃn]	Bestätigung
to effect payment	[ɪˈfekt ˈpeɪmənt]	eine Zahlung leisten
free domicile	[friː ˈdɑmɪsaɪl]	frei Haus
quotation	[kwəʊˈteɪʃn]	Preisangebot
recipient	[rɪˈsɪpɪənt]	Abnehmer/-in, Empfänger/-in
storage capacity	[ˈstɔːrɪdʒ kəˈpæsətɪ]	Lagerkapazität

UNIT 5

WORD BANK 1

abroad	[əˈbrɔːd]	Ausland, ins Ausland
to depend on	[dɪˈpend ɒn]	abhängig sein von
exploitation	[ˌeksplɔɪˈteɪʃn]	Ausbeutung, Ausnutzung
extent	[ɪkˈstent]	Ausmaß, Umfang
feature	[ˈfiːtʃə]	Merkmal
Gross Domestic Product (GPD)	[grəʊs dəʊˈmestɪk ˈprɒdʌkt]	Bruttoinlandsprodukt
interdependence	[ˌɪntədɪˈpendəns]	Abhängigkeit, Wechselbeziehung
literally	[ˈlɪtərəlɪ]	wortwörtlich
origin	[ˈɒrɪdʒɪn]	Ursprung
to outsource	[ˈaʊtsɔːs]	ausgliedern
questionnaire	[ˌkwestʃəˈneə]	Fragebogen
to set up	[set ʌp]	arrangieren
to shift	[ʃɪft]	verlagern
shortage	[ˈʃɔːtɪdʒ]	Mangel
to span	[spæn]	umfassen, umspannen

Word Banks

WORD BANK 2

containerisation	[kənˈteɪnəriːseɪʃn]	Container-Transport
corporate image	[ˈkɔːpərət ˈɪmɪdʒ]	Firmenbild
decade	[ˈdekeɪd]	Jahrzehnt
to perform	[pəˈfɔːm]	auftreten, durchführen
revenue	[ˈrevənjuː]	Umsatz
to take advantage of	[teɪk ədˈvɑːntɪdʒ əv]	einen Vorteil aus etwas ziehen
trade barrier	[treɪd ˈbærɪə]	Handelsschranke
transport operator	[ˈtrænsɔːt ˈɒpəreɪtə]	Transportunternehmer
ultimate goal	[ˈʌltɪmət gəʊl]	Endziel

WORD BANK 3

to accompany	[əˈkʌmpəni]	begleiten, beifügen
bill of lading	[bɪl əv ˈleɪdɪŋ]	Frachtbrief
commercial invoice	[kəˈmɜːʃl ˈɪnvɔɪs]	Warenrechnung
freight forwarder	[freɪt ˈfɔːwədə]	Spediteur
grade	[greɪd]	Grad, Anspruchsklasse
parcel label	[ˈpɑːsl leɪbl]	Paketaufkleber
proof	[pruːf]	Beweis, Abzug
to reject	[ˈriːdʒekt]	abweisen, ablehnen
seagoing vessel	[ˈsiːˌgəʊɪŋ ˈvesl]	Seeschiff
to serve	[sɜːv]	dienen, nützen

WORD BANK 4

apology	[əˈpɒlədʒɪ]	Entschuldigung
breakage	[ˈbreɪkɪdʒ]	Bruch
complaint	[kəmˈpleɪnt]	Beschwerde
evidence	[ˈevɪdəns]	Beweis
faulty	[ˈfɔːltɪ]	fehlerhaft
imprint	[ɪmˈprɪnt]	Eindruck, Abdruck
insufficient	[ˌɪnsəˈfɪʃnt]	unzureichend
jar	[dʒɑː]	Glas(gefäß)
padding	[ˈpædɪŋ]	Auspolsterung, Füllmaterial
replacement	[rɪˈpleɪsmənt]	Ersatz
scratched	[skrætʃt]	verkratzt

Alphabetical Word List: English – German

A

abroad	[əˈbrɔːd] 4	Ausland, ins Ausland
to accelerate	[əkˈseləreɪt] 1, 4	zunehmen
to accompany	[əˈkʌmpənɪ] 5	begleiten, beifügen
accounting department	[əˈkaʊntŋ dɪˈpɑːtmənt] 3	Buchhaltung
additional	[əˈdɪʃ(ə)nəl] 4	zusätzlich
adjustment	[əˈdʒʌstmənt] 5	Anpassung, Schadensregelung
advice	[ədˈvaɪs] 3	Rat, Empfehlung
air waybill	[ˈeə weɪbɪl] 3	Luftfrachtbrief
aisle	[aɪl] 4	Gang, Mittelgang
ample	[ˈæmpl] 2	geräumig, ausgiebig
ankle	[ˈæŋkl] 2	Fußgelenk, Fußknöchel
apology	[əˈpɒlədʒɪ] 5	Entschuldigung
apparently	[əˈpærəntlɪ] 3	anscheinend, augenscheinlich
to appreciate	[əˈpriːʃɪeɪt] 4	zu schätzen wissen, begrüßen
apprentice	[əˈprentɪs] 1	Auszubildende/-r, Lehrling
apprenticeship	[əˈprentɪʃɪp] 1, 4	Ausbildungsplatz
appropriate	[əˈprəʊprɪeɪt] 3	angemessen
to arrange	[əˈreɪndʒ] 1	ausmachen, arrangieren
as a result	[əz ə rɪˈzʌlt] 3	schlussfolgernd
average	[ˈæv(ə)rɪdʒ] 4	Durchschnitt
to avoid	[əˈvɔɪd] 2	verhindern

B

bay	[beɪ] 4	Bucht, Laderaum
to be tied up	[biː taɪd ʌp] 1	beschäftigt sein
to become familiar with	[bɪˈkʌm fəˈŋɪljə wɪð] 2	mit etwas vertraut werden
to become redundant	[bɪˈkʌm rɪˈdʌndənt] 4	seinen Arbeitsplatz verlieren
billion	[ˈbɪljən] 4	Milliarde
bill of lading	[bɪl əv ˈleɪdɪŋ] 5	Frachtbrief
breakage	[ˈbreɪkɪdʒ] 5	Bruch
briefing	[briːfɪŋ] 1	Einsatzbesprechung
bruise	[bruːz] 2	Prellung, Bluterguss
to bump into sth./so.	[bʌmp ˈɪntʊ] 2	mit etwas/jemandem zusammenstoßen
by heart	[baɪ hɑːt] 3	auswendig

C

carrier	[ˈkærɪə] 3	Frachtführer
to check	[tʃæk] 3	prüfen
cold storage	[kəʊld ˈstɔːrɪdʒ] 4	Kühllager
commercial invoice	[kəˈmɜːʃl ˈɪnvɔɪs] 5	Warenrechnung
common	[ˈkɒmən] 2	alltäglich, häufig, bekannt

Alphabetical Word List: English – German

compensation	[ˌkɑmpenˈseɪʃn] 2	Schmerzensgeld, Schadensersatz
competition	[ˌkɒmpɪˈtɪʃn] 5	Wettbewerb
competitive	[kəmˈpetətɪv] 3	wettbewerbsfähig
to complain	[kəmˈpleɪn] 3	reklamieren, sich beschweren
complaint	[kəmˈpleɪnt] 5	Beschwerde
concrete floor	[kənˈkriːt flɔː] 2	Betonboden
condition	[kənˈdɪʃn] 3	Zustand
confirmation	[ˌkɒnfəˈmeɪʃn] 4	Bestätigung
to consider	[kənˈsɪdə] 3	in Erwägung ziehen, betrachten
considerable	[kənˈsɪd(ə)rəb(ə)l] 1	beträchtlich, beachtlich
consignment/delivery/shipment	[kənˈsaɪnmənt/dɪˈlɪvərɪ/ˈʃɪpmənt] 3	Lieferung
containerisation	[kənˈteɪnəriːseɪʃn] 5	Container-Transport
to contribute	[kənˈtrɪbjuːt] 4	beisteuern, einen Beitrag leisten
convenience	[kənˈviːnjəns] 4	Bequemlichkeit, Verbraucherfreundlichkeit
corporate image	[ˈkɔːpərət ˈɪmɪdʒ] 5	Firmenbild
to correspond	[ˌkɒrɪˈspɒnd tuː] 3	etwas entsprechen
counterintuitive	[ˌkaʊnt(ə)rɪnˈtjuːɪtɪv] 4	widersinnig
to crush	[krʌʃ] 2	quetschen, zerdrücken
curriculum vitae	[kəˌrɪkjʊləm ˈviːtaɪ] 4	Lebenslauf
customised	[ˈkʌstəmaɪzd] 1	kundenspezifisch
cutlery	[ˈkʌtləri] 5	Besteck

D

decade	[ˈdekeɪd] 5	Jahrzehnt
decarbonisation	[diːˈkɑ(r)bəniːseɪʃn] 4	Reduzierung von CO_2-Emissionen
to decrease	[ˈdiːkriːs] 4	fallen
dedicated	[ˈdedɪkeɪtɪd] 1	engagiert
delicate	[ˈdelɪkət] 5	heikel
delivery date	[dɪˈlɪvərɪ deɪt] 2	Liefertermin
delivery note	[dɪˈlɪvərɪ nəʊt] 3	Lieferschein
delivery time	[dɪˈlɪvərɪ taɪm] 3	Lieferzeitpunkt, Lieferfrist
demand	[dɪˈmɑːnd] 4	Nachfrage
demanding	[dɪˈmɑːndɪŋ] 1	fordernd
to depend on	[dɪˈpend ɒn] 5	abhängig sein von
discount	[ˈdɪskaʊnt] 2	Rabatt, Ermäßigung
to dispatch	[dɪˈspætʃ] 4	verschicken
to dispose	[dɪˈspəʊz] 3	entsorgen
distribution	[ˈdɪstrɪbjuːtɪŋ] 4	Versand
to document	[ˈdɒkjʊmənt] 3	beurkunden, dokumentieren
drive technology	[draɪv tekˈnɒlədʒi] 4	Antriebstechnologie

Alphabetical Word List: English – German

E

economy	[ɪˈkɒnəmi] 4	Wirtschaft
to effect	[ɪˈfekt] 4	ausführen, durchführen
to effect payment	[ɪˈfekt ˈpeɪmənt] 4	eine Zahlung leisten
(electronic) order picking	[ˌɪlekˈtrɒnɪkˈɔːdə ˈpɪkɪŋ] 4	(beleglose) Kommisionierung
employee	[ˌemplɔɪˈi] 1	Mitarbeiter/-in
employer	[ɪmˈplɔɪə] 1	Arbeitgeber/-in
to encourage	[ɪnˈkʌrɪdʒ] 4	ermuntern
engineer	[ˌendʒɪˈbɪə] 1	Techniker/-in
enquiry	[ɪnˈkwaɪərɪ] 3	Anfrage
entire	[ɪnˈtaɪəstɑːf] 2	ganz, komplett
essential	[ɪˈsenʃl] 4	notwendig, grundlegend
to establish	[ɪˈstæblɪʃ] 1	errichten, gründen
evidence	[ˈevɪdəns] 5	Beweis
to exceed	[ɪkˈsiːd] 2	übertreffen
to exchange sth.	[ɪksˈtʃeɪndʒ] 3	etwas austauschen
to expand	[ɪkˈspænd] 1	expandieren, erweitern
expectation	[ˌekspekˈteɪzn] 5	Erwartung
exploitation	[ˌeksplɔɪˈteɪʃn] 5	Ausbeutung, Ausnutzung
extent	[ɪkˈstent] 5	Ausmaß, Umfang

F

to facilitate	[fəˈsɪlɪteɪt] 4	erleichtern
factory	[ˈfæktri] 1	Fabrik
fatality	[fəˈtæləti] 2	Unglück, Todesfall
faulty	[ˈfɔːlti] 5	fehlerhaft
favourable	[ˈfeɪvərəbl] 3	günstig
feasibility	[ˌfiːzəˈbɪləti] 4	Machbarkeit
feature	[ˈfiːtʃə] 5	Merkmal
filing cabinet	[ˈfaɪlɪŋ ˈkæbɪnɪt] 3	Aktenschrank
fire hazard	[ˈfaɪə(r) ˈhæzə(r)d] 4	Brandgefahr
fireproof	[ˈfaɪəpruːf] 2	feuerfest, feuerbeständig
fire safety	[ˈfaɪə(r) ˈseɪfti] 4	Brandschutz
first of all	[fɜːst əv ɔːl] 3	zuerst, zuallererst
to flourish	[ˈflʌrɪʃ] 1	florieren
forwarding documents	[ˈfɔːwədɪŋ ˈdɒkjʊmənts] 3	Warenbegleitpapiere
founder	[ˈfaʊndə] 1	Gründer/-in
free domicile	[friː ˈdɑmɪsaɪl] 4	frei Haus
freight forwarder	[freɪt ˈfɔːwədə] 5	Spediteur
freight forwarding industry	[freɪt ˈfɔːwədɪŋ ˈɪndəstri] 4	Speditionsbranche
furthermore	[ˌfɜːðəˈmɔː] 3	außerdem, darüber hinaus

G/H

to gain	[geɪn] 3	erlangen, aneignen
goods issue	[gʊdz ˈɪʃjuː] 1	Warenausgang

Alphabetical Word List: English – German

goods receipt	[gʊdz rɪˈsiːt] 1	Wareneingang
goods receipt slip	[gʊdz rɪˈsiːt slɪp] 3	Wareneingangsschein
grade	[greɪd] 5	Grad, Anspruchsklasse
to grant	[grɑːnt] 2	gewähren, einräumen
grateful	[ˈgreɪtfʊl] 2	dankbar
groceries	[ˈgrəʊsərɪz] 1	Lebensmittel
Gross Domestic Product (GPD)	[grəʊs dəʊˈmestɪk ˈprɒdʌkt] 5	Bruttoinlandsprodukt
growth	[grəʊθ] 1	Wachstum
hazard	[ˈhæzəd] 2	Gefahr, Risiko
humble	[ˈhʌmb(ə)l] 1	bescheiden
hydrogen	[ˈhaɪdrədʒən] 4	Wasserstoff

I/J/K

impact	[ˈɪmpækt] 5	Einfluss, Auswirkung
imprint	[ɪmˈprɪnt] 5	Eindruck, Abdruck
in addition	[ɪn əˈdɪʃn] 3	ergänzend, hinzu kommt
to inaugurate	[ɪˈnɔːgjʊreɪt] 1	einweihen
in my opinion	[ɪn maɪ əˈpɪnjən] 3	meiner Meinung nach
inconvenience	[ˌɪnkənˈviːnjəns] 5	Unannehmlichkeit
to increase	[ɪnˈkriːs] 4	steigen
injury	[ˈɪndʒərɪ] 2	Verwundung, Verletzung
inspection	[ɪnˈspekʃən] 2	Prüfung, Kontrolle
in stock	[ɪn stɒk] 3	auf Lager, vorrätig
insufficient	[ˌɪnsəˈfɪʃnt] 5	unzureichend
to intend	[ɪnˈtend] 4	beabsichtigen, anstreben
interdependence	[ˌɪntədɪˈpendəns] 5	Abhängigkeit, Wechselbeziehung
interface	[ˌɪntəˈfeɪs] 3	Schnittstelle
in turn	[ɪn ˈtɜː(r)n] 1	wiederum
invoice	[ˈɪnvɔɪs] 3	Rechnung
issue	[ˈɪʃuː] 5	Angelegenheit
jar	[dʒɑː] 5	Glas(gefäß)
to kneel down	[niːl daʊn] 2	sich hinknien

L

label	[ˈleɪbl] 4	Etikett, Aufkleber
last but not least	[lɑːst bʌt nɑt liːst] 3	nicht zuletzt
life cycle	[ˈlaɪf ˈsʌɪkl] 4	Lebensdauer
literally	[ˈlɪtərəlɪ] 5	wortwörtlich
located	[ləʊˈkeɪtɪd] 3	ansässig
location	[ləʊˈkeɪʃn] 1	Standort
logistics	[ləˈdʒɪstɪks] 4	Versorgung, Logistik
to look forward to doing sth.	[lʊk ˈfɔːwəd tuː] 1	sich darauf freuen, etwas zu tun

Alphabetical Word List: English – German

low level order picking	[ləʊ ˌlevl' ɔːdə' pɪkɪŋ] 4	maschinengestützte Kommissionierung
luggage	[ˈlʌgɪdʒ] 3	Gepäck

M/N

to maintain sth.	[meɪnˈteɪn] 4	etwas aufrecht erhalten
to manage sth.	[ˈmænɪdʒ] 1	es schaffen, etwas zu tun
mandatory	[ˈmændətərɪ] 2	verpflichtend
manual handling	[ˈmænjʊəl ˈhændlɪŋ] 2	manuelle Handhabung
marketer	[ˈmɑːkɪtə] 4	Vermarkter
measure	[ˌmeʒə] 2	Maßnahme
medium-sized	[ˈmiːdjəm saɪzd] 3	mittelständisch
narrow	[ˈnærəʊ] 4	eng, schmal
novice	[ˈnɒvɪs] 2	Anfänger/-in, Neuling

O

to obey	[əˈbeɪ] 3	befolgen, gehorchen
to occur	[əˈkɜː] 2	auftreten
odd	[ɒd] 2	seltsam
offer	[ˈɒfə] 3	Angebot
to omit	[əˈmɪt] 3	weglassen
on the one hand, on the other hand	[ɒn ðə wʌn hænd, ɒn ðiː ˈʌðə hænd] 3	auf der einen Seite, auf der anderen Seite
order	[ˈɔːdə] 3	Auftrag
order picking by pick list	[ˈɔːdə ˈpɪkɪŋ baɪ pɪk lɪst] 4	beleghafte Kommissionierung
organic food	[ɔːˈgænɪk fuːd] 1	Biolebensmittel
origin	[ˈɒrɪdʒɪn] 5	Ursprung
to outsource	[ˈaʊtsɔːs] 5	ausgliedern
owner	[ˈəʊnə] 1	Eigentümer/-in

P/Q

packing list	[ˈpækɪŋ lɪst] 3	Packliste
padding	[ˈpædɪŋ] 5	Auspolsterung, Füllmaterial
pallet	[ˈpælɪt] 3	Palette
parcel label	[ˈpɑːsl leɪbl] 5	Paketaufkleber
to perform	[pəˈfɔːm] 5	auftreten, durchführen
pick-by-barcode	[pɪk baɪ bɑːkəʊd] 4	Kommissionieren per Strichcode
pick-by-light	[pɪk baɪ laɪt] 4	Kommissionieren per LED-Anzeige
pick-by-vision	[pɪkbaɪˈvɪʒn] 4	Kommissionieren per Datenbrille
pick-by-voice	[pɪk baɪ vɔɪs] 4	Kommissionieren per Sprachbefehl
to pinpoint	[ˈpɪnpɔɪnt] 2	genau bestimmen, festlegen
point of sale	[pɔɪnt əv seɪl] 4	Kasse, Verkaufsplatz

Alphabetical Word List: English – German

posture	[ˈpɒstʃə] 2	Haltung, Körperhaltung
precautions	[prɪˈkɔːʃnz] 2	Vorsichtsmaßnahmen
to preserve sth.	[prɪˈzɜːv] 4	etwas aufbewahren
to prevent	[prɪˈvent] 4	vermeiden
processing	[ˈprəʊsesɪŋ] 1, 5	Bearbeitung, Verarbeitung
product line	[ˈprɒdʌkt laɪn] 1	Sortiment
to prohibit	[prəˈhɪbɪt] 2	verbieten
proof	[pruːf] 5	Beweis, Abzug
to protect from	[prəˈtekt frɒm] 3	schützen vor
to provide	[prəˈvaɪd] 4	bereitstellen, anbieten
to provide with	[prəˈvaɪd wɪð] 1	versorgen mit
to purchase	[ˈpɜːtʃəs] 1	(ein)kaufen
purchasing department	[ˈpɜːtʃəsɪŋ dɪˈpɑːtmənt] 3	Einkaufsabteilung
quality control department	[ˈkwɒlətɪ kənˈtrəʊl dɪˈpɑːtmənt] 3	Qualitätskontrolle
questionnaire	[ˌkwestʃəˈneə] 5	Fragebogen
quotation	[kwəʊˈteɪʃn] 4	Preisangebot

R

range of	[reɪndʒ əv] 2	Auswahl/Angebot an
reasonable	[ˈriːznəbl] 1	vernünftig
receipt	[rɪˈsiːt] 4	Erhalt, Eingang
recipient	[rɪˈsɪpɪənt] 4	Abnehmer/-in, Empfänger/-in
to redecorate	[riːˈdekəreɪt] 3	renovieren
to reduce	[rɪˈdjuːs] 4	verringern
refrigerated freight	[rɪˈfrɪdʒəreɪtɪd freɪt] 4	Kühltransport
to reject	[ˈriːdʒekt] 5	abweisen, ablehnen
relocation	[riːləʊˈkeɪʃn] 1	Umzug/Verlegung
to rephrase	[rɪˈfreɪz] 2	umformulieren
replacement	[rɪˈpleɪsmənt] 5	Ersatz
requirement	[rɪˈkwaɪəmənt] 2	Anforderung
resource	[rɪˈsɔːs] 1	Mittel
retail	[ˈriːteɪl] 1	Einzelhandel
reusable	[ˌriːˈjuːsəbl] 3	wieder verwendbar, Mehrweg-
to reuse	[ˌriːˈjuːs] 4	wiederverwenden
revenue	[ˈrevənjuː] 5	Umsatz

S

safety equipment	[ˈseɪfti ɪˈkwɪpmənt] 4	Sicherheitsausrüstung
safety regulations	[ˈseɪfti ˌregjʊˈleɪʃ(ə)nz] 4	Sicherheitsvorschriften
satisfactory	[ˌsætɪsˈfæktərɪ] 4	zufriedenstellend
schedule	[ˈskedjuːl] 1	Zeitplan
scratched	[skrætʃt] 5	verkratzt
seagoing vessel	[ˈsiːˌgəʊɪŋ ˈvesl] 5	Seeschiff
to sell	[sel] 4	verkaufen
to serve	[sɜːv] 5	dienen, nützen

Alphabetical Word List: English – German

English	Pronunciation	German
to set up	[set ʌp] 5	arrangieren
severe	[sɪˈvɪə] 2	ernst, schlimm, schwer
shelf life	[ʃelf laɪf] 4	Haltbarkeit
to shift	[ʃɪft] 5	verlagern
shortage	[ˈʃɔːtɪdʒ] 1, 5	Mangel
to sign a receipt	[saɪn ə rɪˈsiːt] 3	eine Quittung unterschreiben
slips and trips	[slɪps ænd trɪps] 2	Ausrutschen und Stolpern
smoothly	[smuːðlɪ] 1	glatt, ohne Probleme
to span	[spæn] 5	umfassen, umspannen
to stack	[stæk] 4	aufschichten, stapeln
staff	[staːf] 1	Belegschaft, Mitarbeiter
steering	[ˈstɪərɪŋ] 4	Lenkung, Steuerung
stock	[stɒk] 1	Lager
stock list	[ˈstɒk lɪst] 3	Lagerliste
stocktaking	[ˈstɒkˌteɪkɪŋ] 4	Inventur
storage	[ˈstɔːrɪdʒ] 4	Einlagerung
storage area	[ˈstɔːrɪdʒ ˈeərɪə] 4	Lagerfläche
storage capacity	[ˈstɔːrɪdʒ kəˈpæsətɪ] 4	Lagerkapazität
stress	[stres] 4	Belastung, Druck
to submit	[səbˈmɪt] 4	unterbreiten
subsidiary	[səbˈsɪdjərɪ] 1	Niederlassung
substantial	[səbˈstænʃl] 2	umfangreich, beträchtlich
success	[səkˈses] 1	Erfolg
to suggest	[səˈdʒest] 1	vorschlagen
to sum it up	[sʌm ɪt ʌp] 3	um es zusammenzufassen
support	[səˈpɔːt] 1	Unterstützung
sustainability	[səˈsteɪnəˈbɪlətɪ] 4	Nachhaltigkeit

T

to take advantage of	[teɪk ədˈvɑːntɪdʒ əv] 5	einen Vorteil aus etwas ziehen
to take over	[teɪk ˈəʊvə(r)] 1	übernehmen
terms of delivery	[tɜːmz əv dɪˈlɪvərɪ] 2	Lieferbedingungen
terms of payment	[tɜːmz əv ˈpeɪmənt] 2	Zahlungsbedingungen
theft	[θeft] 2	Diebstahl
therefore	[ˈðeəfɔː] 3	somit, deshalb
threat	[θret] 2	Drohung, Gefährdung
time consuming	[taɪm kənˈsjuːmɪŋ] 4	zeitaufwändig
trade barrier	[treɪd ˈbærɪə] 5	Handelsschranke
transport operator	[ˈtrænsɔːt ˈɒpəreɪtə] 5	Transportunternehmer

U/V/W

ultimate goal	[ˈʌltɪmət ɡəʊl] 5	Endziel
to unload sth.	[ˌʌnˈləʊd] 3	etwas abladen
vacancy	[ˈveɪkənsɪ] 1	offene Arbeitsstelle
vermin	[ˈvɜːmɪn] 3	Schädlinge

Alphabetical Word List: English – German

walk through	[wɔ:k θru:] 2	Rundgang, Ortsbesichtigung
warehouse administration	[ˈweəhaʊz ədˌmɪnɪˈstreɪʃn] 1	Lagerverwaltung
warehouse industry	[ˈweəhaʊz ˈɪndəstri] 4	Lagerbranche
warehouse operator	[ˈweəhaʊz ˈɒpəreɪtə] 1	Fachlagerist/-in
warehouse supervisor	[ˈweəhaʊz ˈsu:pəvaɪzə] 1	Lagerleiter/-in
whereas	[weərˈæz] 3	wobei, wohingegen
while	[waɪl] 3	während
wholesaler	[ˈhəʊlˌseɪlə] 1	Großhändler
workplace	[ˈwɜ:kˈpleɪs] 1	Arbeitsplatz

@/.../!

(…)	in brackets	[ɪn ˈbrækɪts]	in Klammern
(	open bracket	[ˈəʊpən ˈbrækɪt]	Klammer auf
)	close bracket	[kləʊz ˈbrækɪt]	Klammer zu
/	slash	[slæʃ]	Schrägstrich
–	dash	[dæʃ]	Gedankenstrich
_	underscore	[ˌʌndə(r)ˈskɔ:(r)]	Unterstrich
@	at	[æt]	at
.	dot (in e-mails)	[dɒt]	Punkt

Alphabetical Word List: German – English

A

abhängig sein von	to depend on [dɪˈpend ɒn] 5
Abhängigkeit	interdependence [ˌɪntədɪˈpendəns] 5
abladen: etwas abl.	to unload sth. [ˌʌnˈləʊd] 3
ablehnen	to reject [ˈriːdʒekt] 5
Abnehmer/-in	recipient [rɪˈsɪpɪənt] 4
Abzug	proof [pruːf] 5
Aktenschrank	filing cabinet [ˈfaɪlɪŋ ˈkæbɪnɪt] 3
alltäglich	common [ˈkɒmən] 2
Anfänger/-in	novice [ˈnɒvɪs] 2
Anforderung	requirement [rɪˈkwaɪəmənt] 2
Anfrage	enquiry [ɪnˈkwaɪərɪ] 3
Angebot	offer [ˈɒfə] 3
Angelegenheit	issue [ˈɪʃuː] 5
angemessen	appropriate [əˈprəʊprɪeɪt] 3
Anpassung	adjustment [əˈdʒʌstmənt] 5
ansässig	located [ləʊˈkeɪtɪd] 3
anscheinend	apparently [əˈpærəntlɪ] 3
Antriebstechnologie	drive technology [draɪv tekˈnɒlədʒi] 4
Arbeitgeber	employer [ɪmˈplɔɪə] 1
Arbeitsplatz	workplace [ˈwɜːkˈpleɪs] 1
arrangieren	to set up [set ʌp] 5, to arrange [əˈreɪndʒ] 1
Aufkleber	label [ˈleɪbl] 4
auf Lager (vorrätig)	in stock [ɪn stɒk] 3
aufschichten	to stack [stæk] 4
aufrecht erhalten, etwas aufr. erh.	to maintain sth. [meɪnˈteɪn] 4
Auftrag	order [ˈɔːdə] 3
auftreten	to occur [əˈkɜː] 2
Ausbeutung	exploitation [ˌeksplɔɪˈteɪʃn] 5
Ausbildung(splatz)	apprenticeship [əˈprentɪʃɪp] 1
ausführen	to effect [ɪˈfekt] 4
ausgliedern	to outsource [ˈaʊtsɔːs] 5
Ausland, ins Ausland	abroad [əˈbrɔːd] 4
Ausmaß	extent [ɪkˈstent] 5
Auspolsterung	padding [ˈpædɪŋ] 5
Ausrutschen und Stolpern	slips and trips [slɪps ænd trɪps] 2
außerdem	furthermore [ˌfɜːðəˈmɔː] 3
Auswahl	range of [reɪndʒ əv] 2
auswendig	by heart [baɪ hɑːt] 3
Auszubildende/-in	apprentice [əˈprentɪs] 1

B

beabsichtigen, anstreben	to intend [ɪnˈtend] 4
Bearbeitung	processing [ˈprəʊsesɪŋ] 1, 5
befolgen	to obey [əˈbeɪ] 3

Alphabetical Word List: German – English

begleiten	to accompany [əˈkʌmpəni] 5
beisteuern	to contribute [kənˈtrɪbjuːt] 4
Belastung	stress [stres] 4
Belegschaft	staff [stɑːf] 1
Bequemlichkeit	convenience [kənˈviːnjəns] 4
bereitstellen, anbieten	to provide [prəˈvaɪd] 4
beschäftigt sein	to be tied up [biː taɪd ʌp] 1
bescheiden	humble [ˈhʌmb(ə)l] 1
Beschwerde	complaint [kəmˈpleɪnt] 5
beschweren: sich beschw.	to complain [kəmˈpleɪn] 3
Bestätigung	confirmation [ˌkɑnfəˈmeɪʃn] 4
Besteck	cutlery [ˈkʌtləri] 5
Betonboden	concrete floor [kənˈkriːt flɔː] 2
beträchtlich, beachtlich	considerable [kənˈsɪd(ə)rəb(ə)l] 1
beurkunden	to document [ˈdɒkjʊmənt] 3
Beweis	evidence [ˈevɪdəns] 5
Biolebensmittel	organic food [ɔːˈɡænɪk fuːd] 1
Brandgefahr	fire hazard [ˈfaɪə(r) ˈhæzə(r)d] 4
Brandschutz	fire safety [ˈfaɪə(r) ˈseɪfti] 4
Bruch	breakage [ˈbreɪkɪdʒ] 5
Bruttoinlandsprodukt	Gross Domestic Product (GPD) [ɡrəʊs dəʊˈmestɪk ˈprɒdʌkt] 5
Buchhaltung	accounting department [əˈkaʊntɪŋ dɪˈpɑːtmənt] 3
Bucht (Laderaum)	bay [beɪ] 4

C/D

Container-Transport	containerisation [kənˈteɪnəriːseɪʃn] 5
dankbar	grateful [ˈɡreɪtfʊl] 2
Diebstahl	theft [θeft] 2
dienen	to serve [sɜːv] 5
Drohung	threat [θret] 2
Druck	stress [stres] 4
Durchschnitt	average [ˈæv(ə)rɪdʒ] 4

E

Eigentümer/-in	owner [ˈəʊnə] 1
Eindruck (Abdruck)	imprint [ɪmˈprɪnt] 5
Einfluss	impact [ˈɪmpækt] 5
Eingang	receipt [rɪˈsiːt] 4
Einkaufsabteilung	purchasing department [ˈpɜːtʃəsɪŋ dɪˈpɑːtmənt] 3
Einlagerung	storage [ˈstɔːrɪdʒ] 4
Einsatzbesprechung	briefing [briːfɪŋ] 1
einweihen	to inaugurate [ɪˈnɔːɡjʊreɪt] 1
Einzelhandel	retail [riːˈteɪl] 1
Empfänger/-in	recipient [rɪˈsɪpɪənt] 4
Endziel	ultimate goal [ˈʌltɪmət ɡəʊl] 5

Alphabetical Word List: German – English

eng	narrow [ˈnærəʊ] 4
engagiert	dedicated [ˈdedɪkeɪtɪd] 1
Entschuldigung	apology [əˈpɒlədʒɪ] 5
entsorgen	to dispose [dɪˈspəʊz] 3
entsprechen, etwas entspr.	to correspond [ˌkɒrɪˈspɒnd tuː] 3
Erfolg	success [səkˈses] 1
ergänzend (hinzu kommt)	in addition [ɪn əˈdɪʃn] 3
erlangen	to gain [geɪn] 3
erleichtern	to facilitate [fəˈsɪlɪteɪt] 4
ermuntern	to encourage [ɪnˈkʌrɪdʒ] 4
ernst	severe [sɪˈvɪə] 2
errichten, gründen	to establish [ɪˈstæblɪʃ] 1
Ersatz	replacement [rɪˈpleɪsmənt] 5
Erwartung	expectation [ˌekspekˈteɪzn] 5
erwägen: in Erwägung ziehen	to consider [kənˈsɪdə] 3
Etikett	label [ˈleɪbl] 4
expandieren, erweitern	to expand [ɪkˈspænd] 1

F

Fabrik	factory [ˈfæktrɪ] 1
Fachlagerist/-in	warehouse operator [ˈweəhaʊz ˈɒpəreɪtə] 1
fallen	to decrease [ˈdiːkriːs] 4
fehlerhaft	faulty [ˈfɔːltɪ] 5
festlegen	to pinpoint [ˈpɪnpɔɪnt] 2
feuerfest, feuerbeständig	fireproof [ˈfaɪəpruːf] 2
Firmenbild	corporate image [ˈkɔːpərət ˈɪmɪdʒ] 5
florieren	to flourish [ˈflʌrɪʃ] 1
fordernd	demanding [dɪˈmɑːndɪŋ] 1
Frachtbrief	bill of lading [bɪl əv ˈleɪdɪŋ] 5
Frachtführer	carrier [ˈkærɪə] 3
Fragebogen	questionnaire [ˌkwestʃəˈneə] 5
frei Haus	free domicile [friː ˈdɑmɪsaɪl] 4
Füllmaterial	padding [ˈpædɪŋ] 5
Fußgelenk, Fußknöchel	ankle [ˈæŋkl] 2

G

Gang	aisle [aɪl] 4
ganz (komplett)	entire [ɪnˈtaɪə] 2
Gefahr	hazard [ˈhæzəd] 2
Gepäck	luggage [ˈlʌgɪdʒ] 3
geräumig	ample [ˈæmpl] 2
gewähren	to grant [grɑːnt] 2
Glas(gefäß)	jar [dʒɑː] 5
glatt	smoothly [smuːðlɪ] 1
Grad	grade [greɪd] 5
Großhändler	wholesaler [ˈhəʊlˌseɪlə] 1

Alphabetical Word List: German – English

Gründer/-in	founder [ˈfaʊndə] 1
günstig	favourable [ˈfeɪvərəbl] 3

H

Haltbarkeit	shelf life [ʃelf laɪf] 4
Haltung (Körperhaltung)	posture [ˈpɒstʃə] 2
Handelsschranke	trade barrier [treɪd ˈbærɪə] 5
heikel	delicate [ˈdelɪkət] 5

I/J

Inventur	stocktaking [ˈstɒkˌteɪkɪŋ] 4
Jahrzehnt	decade [ˈdekeɪd] 5

K

Kasse	point of sale [pɔɪnt əv seɪl] 4
kaufen, einkaufen	to purchase [pɜːtʃəs] 1
Kommissionieren per Datenbrille	pick-by-vision [pɪkbaɪˈvɪʒn] 4
Kommissionieren per LED-Anzeige	pick-by-light [pɪk baɪ laɪt] 4
Kommissionieren per Sprachbefehl	pick-by-voice [pɪk baɪ vɔɪs] 4
Kommissionieren per Strichcode	pick-by-barcode [pɪk baɪ bɑːkəʊd] 4
Kommisionierung, beleglose	(electronic) order picking [ˌɪlekˈtrɒnɪk ˈɔːdə ˈpɪkɪŋ] 4
Kühllager	cold storage [kəʊld ˈstɔːrɪdʒ] 4
Kühltransport	refrigerated freight [rɪˈfrɪdʒəreɪtɪd freɪt] 4
kundenspezifisch	customised [ˈkʌstəmaɪzd] 1

L

Lager	stock [stɒk] 1
Lagerbranche	warehouse industry [ˈweəhaʊz ˈɪndəstri] 4
Lagerfläche	storage area [ˈstɔːrɪdʒ ˈeərɪə] 4
Lagerkapazität	storage capacity [ˈstɔːrɪdʒ kəˈpæsəti] 4
Lagerleiter/-in	warehouse supervisor [ˈweəhaʊz ˈsuːpəvaɪzə] 1
Lagerliste	stock list [ˈstɒk lɪst] 3
Lagerverwaltung	warehouse administration [ˈweəhaʊz ədˌmɪnɪˈstreɪʃn] 1
Lebensdauer	life cycle [ˈlaɪf ˈsʌɪkl] 4
Lebenslauf	curriculum vitae [kəˌrɪkjʊləm ˈviːtaɪ] 4
Lebensmittel	groceries [ˈgrəʊsərɪz] 1
eine Zahlung leisten	to effect payment [ɪˈfekt ˈpeɪmənt] 4
Lenkung, Steuerung	steering [ˈstɪərɪŋ] 4
Lieferbedingungen	terms of delivery [tɜːmz əv dɪˈlɪvəri] 2
Lieferfrist	delivery time [dɪˈlɪvəriˈtaɪm] 3
Lieferschein	delivery note [dɪˈlɪvəri nəʊt] 3
Liefertermin	delivery date [dɪˈlɪvəri deɪt] 2
Lieferung	consignment/delivery/shipment [kənˈsaɪnmənt/ dɪˈlɪvəri/ ˈʃɪpmənt] 3
Lieferzeitpunkt	delivery time [dɪˈlɪvəriˈtaɪm] 3
Logistik	logistics [ləˈdʒɪstɪks] 4
Luftfrachtbrief	air waybill [ˈeə weɪbɪl] 3

Alphabetical Word List: German – English

M

Machbarkeit	feasibility [ˌfi:zəˈbɪləti] 4
Mangel	shortage [ˈʃɔ:tɪdʒ] 5
manuelle Handhabung	manual handling [ˈmænjʊəl ˈhændlɪŋ] 2
Maßnahme	measure [ˌmeʒə] 2
Meinung: meiner Meinung nach	in my opinion [ɪn maɪ əˈpɪnjən] 3
Merkmal	feature [ˈfi:tʃə] 5
Milliarde	billion [ˈbɪljən] 4
Mitarbeiter/-in	employee [ˌemplɔɪˈi] 1
Mittel	resource [rɪˈsɔ:s] 1
Mittelgang	aisle [aɪl] 4
mittelständisch	medium-sized [ˈmi:djəm saɪzd] 3

N

Nachfrage	demand [dɪˈmɑ:nd] 4
Nachhaltigkeit	sustainability [səˈsteɪnəˈbɪləti] 4
nicht zuletzt	last but not least [lɑ:st bʌt nɑt li:st] 3
Niederlassung	subsidiary [səbˈsɪdjərɪ] 1
notwendig (grundlegend)	essential [ɪˈsenʃl] 4

O/P

offen: offene Arbeitsstelle	vacancy [ˈveɪkənsɪ] 1
Packliste	packing list [ˈpækɪŋ lɪst] 3
Paketaufkleber	parcel label [ˈpɑ:sl leɪbl] 5
Palette	pallet [ˈpælɪt] 3
Preisangebot	quotation [kwəʊˈteɪʃn] 4
Prellung	bruise [brɔu:z] 2
prüfen	to check [tʃæk] 3
Prüfung (Kontrolle)	inspection [ɪnˈspekʃən] 2

Q/R

Qualitätskontrolle	quality control department [ˈkwɒlətɪ kənˈtrəʊl dɪˈpɑ:tmənt] 3
quetschen (zerdrücken)	to crush [krʌʃ] 2
Quittung: eine Qu. unterschreiben	to sign a receipt [saɪn ə rɪˈsi:t] 3
Rabatt	discount [ˈdɪskaʊnt] 2
Rat	advice [ədˈvaɪs] 3
Rechnung	invoice [ˈɪnvɔɪs] 3
Reduzierung von CO_2-Emissionen	decarbonisation [di:ˈkɑ(r)bəni:seɪʃn] 4
reklamieren	to complain [kəmˈpleɪn] 3
renovieren	to redecorate [ri:ˈdekəreɪt] 3
Rundgang	walk through [wɔ:k θru:] 2

S

Schadensersatz	compensation [ˌkɑmpenˈseɪʃn] 2
Schädlinge	vermin [ˈvɜ:mɪn] 3

Alphabetical Word List: German – English

schlussfolgernd	as a result [əz ə rɪˈzʌlt] 3
Schnittstelle	interface [ˌɪntəˈfeɪs] 3
schützen vor	to protect from [prəˈtekt frɒm] 3
Seeschiff	seagoing vessel [ˈsiːˌgəʊɪŋ ˈvesl] 5
seltsam	odd [ɒd] 2
sich darauf freuen, etwas zu tun	to look forward to doing sth. [lʊk ˈfɔːwəd tuː] 1
Sicherheitsausrüstung	safety equipment [ˈseɪfti ɪˈkwɪpmənt] 4
Sicherheitsvorschriften	safety regulations [ˈseɪfti ˌregjʊˈleɪʃ(ə)nz] 4
sich hinknien	to kneel down [niːl daʊn] 2
somit	therefore [ˈðeəfɔː] 3
Sortiment	product line [ˈprɒdʌkt laɪn] 1
Spediteur	freight forwarder [freɪt ˈfɔːwədə] 5
Speditionsbranche	freight forwarding industry [freɪt ˈfɔːwədɪŋ ˈɪndəstri] 4
Standort	location [ləʊˈkeɪʃn] 1
stapeln	to stack [stæk] 4
steigen	to increase [ɪnˈkriːs] 4

T/U

Techniker/-in	engineer [ˌendʒɪˈbɪə] 1
Transportunternehmer	transport operator [ˈtrænsɔːt ˈɒpəreɪtə] 5
übernehmen	to take over [teɪk ˈəʊvə(r)] 1
übertreffen	to exceed [ɪkˈsiːd] 2
umfangreich (beträchtlich)	substantial [səbˈstænʃl] 2
umformulieren	to rephrase [rɪˈfreɪz] 2
Umsatz	revenue [ˈrevənjuː] 5
umspannen	to span [spæn] 5
Umzug/Verlegung	relocation [riːləʊˈkeɪʃn] 1
Unannehmlichkeit	inconvenience [ˌɪnkənˈviːnjəns] 5
Unglück (Todesfall)	fatality [fəˈtælətɪ] 2
unterbreiten	to submit [səbˈmɪt] 4
Unterstützung	support [səˈpɔːt] 1
unzureichend	insufficient [ˌɪnsəˈfɪʃnt] 5
Ursprung	origin [ˈɒrɪdʒɪn] 5

V

verbieten	to prohibit [prəˈhɪbɪt] 2
Verbraucherfreundlichkeit	convenience [kənˈviːnjəns] 4
verhindern	to avoid [əˈvɔɪd] 2
verkaufen	to sell [sel] 4
verkratzt	scratched [skrætʃt] 5
verlagern	to shift [ʃɪft] 5
Vermarkter	marketer [ˈmɑːkɪtə] 4
vermeiden	to prevent [prɪˈvent] 4
vernünftig	reasonable [ˈriːznəbl] 1
verpflichtend	mandatory [ˈmændətərɪ] 2
verringern	to reduce [rɪˈdjuːs] 4

Alphabetical Word List: German – English

Versand	distribution [ˈdɪstrɪbjuːtɪŋ] 4
verschicken	to dispatch [dɪˈspætʃ] 4
versorgen mit	to provide with [prəˈvaɪd wɪð] 1
Verwundung (Verletzung)	injury [ˈɪndʒərɪ] 2
vorschlagen	to suggest [səˈdʒest] 1
Vorsichtsmaßnahmen	precautions [prɪˈkɔːʃnz] 2

W

Wachstum	growth [grəʊθ] 1
während	while [waɪl] 3
Warenausgang	goods issue [gʊdz ˈɪʃjuː] 1
Warenbegleitpapiere	forwarding documents [ˈfɔːwədɪŋ ˈdɒkjʊmənts] 3
Wareneingang	goods receipt [gʊdz rɪˈsiːt] 1
Wareneingangsschein	goods receipt slip [gʊdz rɪˈsiːt slɪp] 3
Warenrechnung	commercial invoice [kəˈmɜːʃl ˈɪnvɔɪs] 5
Wasserstoff	hydrogen [ˈhaɪdrədʒən] 4
weglassen	to omit [əˈmɪt] 3
Wettbewerb	competition [ˌkɒmpɪˈtɪʃn] 5
wettbewerbsfähig	competitive [kəmˈpetətɪv] 3
widersinnig	counterintuitive [ˌkaʊnt(ə)rɪnˈtjuːɪtɪv] 4
wiederum	in turn [ɪn ˈtɜː(r)n] 1
wieder verwendbar	reusable [ˌriːˈjuːsəbl] 3
wiederverwenden	to reuse [ˌriːˈjuːs] 4
Wirtschaft	economy [ɪˈkɒnəmɪ] 4
wortwörtlich	literally [ˈlɪtərəlɪ] 5

Z

Zahlungsbedingungen	terms of payment [tɜːmz əv ˈpeɪmənt] 2
zeitaufwändig	time consuming [taɪm kənˈsjuːmɪŋ] 4
Zeitplan	schedule [ˈskedjuːl] 1
zusammenstoßen: mit etw./jem. z.	to bump into sth./so. [bʌmp ˈɪntʊ] 2
zuerst (zuallererst)	first of all [fɜːst əv ɔːl] 3
zufriedenstellend	satisfactory [ˌsætɪsˈfæktərɪ] 4
zunehmen	to accelerate [əkˈseləreɪt] 1, 4
zusätzlich	additional [əˈdɪʃ(ə)nəl] 4
Zustand	condition [kənˈdɪʃn] 3

@/.../!

(...)	in Klammern	in brackets [ɪn ˈbrækɪts] 1
(	Klammer auf	open bracket [ˈəʊpən ˈbrækɪt] 1
)	Klammer zu	close bracket [kləʊz ˈbrækɪt] 1
/	Schrägstrich	slash [slæʃ] 1
–	Gedankenstrich	dash [dæʃ] 1
_	Unterstrich	underscore [ˌʌndə(r)ˈskɔː(r)] 1
@	at	at [æt] 1
.	Punkt	dot (in e-mails) [dɒt] 1

Irregular Verbs

Infinitive	Simple Past	Past Participle	German
arise	arose	arisen	entstehen, sich erheben
be	was/were	been	sein
bear	bore	borne	(er)tragen
beat	beat	beaten, beat	schlagen
become	became	become	werden
begin	began	begun	beginnen
bend	bent	bent	biegen, beugen
bid	bid	bid	bieten, ein Angebot abgeben
bind	bound	bound	binden, verpflichten
break	broke	broken	(zer)brechen
bring	brought	brought	bringen
build	built	built	bauen
burn	burnt, burned	burnt, burned	brennen, verbrennen
burst	burst	burst	platzen
buy	bought	bought	kaufen
catch	caught	caught	fangen
choose	chose	chosen	wählen
come	came	come	kommen
cost	cost	cost	kosten
cut	cut	cut	schneiden
deal	dealt	dealt	handeln, Geschäfte tätigen
do	did	done	tun, machen
draw	drew	drawn	zeichnen
dream	dreamt, dreamed	dreamt, dreamed	träumen
drink	drank	drunk	trinken
drive	drove	driven	fahren
eat	ate	eaten	essen
fall	fell	fallen	fallen
feel	felt	felt	fühlen
fight	fought	fought	kämpfen
find	found	found	finden
forbid	forbade	forbidden	verbieten, untersagen
forecast	forecast, forecasted	forecast, forecasted	vorhersagen
forget	forgot	forgotten	vergessen
forgive	forgave	forgiven	vergeben, verzeihen
freeze	froze	frozen	einfrieren, gefrieren
get	got	got	bekommen
give	gave	given	geben
go	went	gone	gehen
grow	grew	grown	wachsen
hang	hung	hung	hängen
have	had	had	haben

Irregular Verbs

Infinitive	Simple Past	Past Participle	German
hear	heard	heard	hören
hide	hid	hidden	verstecken
hit	hit	hit	schlagen, hauen
hold	held	held	halten
hurt	hurt	hurt	verletzen
keep	kept	kept	(be)halten, bewahren
kneel	knelt, kneeled	knelt, kneeled	knien
know	knew	known	kennen, wissen
lay	laid	laid	legen
lead	led	led	führen, leiten
lean	leant, leaned	leant, leaned	lehnen
learn	learnt, learned	learnt, learned	lernen
leave	left	left	verlassen
lend	lent	lent	(ver)leihen
let	let	let	lassen
lie	lay	lain	liegen
lose	lost	lost	verlieren
make	made	made	machen, herstellen
mean	meant	meant	meinen, bedeuten
meet	met	met	treffen, begegnen
pay	paid	paid	bezahlen
put	put	put	setzen, stellen, legen
quit	quit, quitted	quit, quitted	beenden, verlassen
read	read	read	lesen
ride	rode	ridden	reiten, fahren (Rad)
rise	rose	risen	(an)steigen, aufgehen
run	ran	run	laufen
say	said	said	sagen
see	saw	seen	sehen
seek	sought	sought	suchen
sell	sold	sold	verkaufen
send	sent	sent	senden, verschicken
shake	shook	shaken	schütteln
show	showed	shown, showed	zeigen
shrink	shrank, shrunk	shrunk	schrumpfen, einlaufen
shut	shut	shut	schließen
sing	sang	sung	singen
sink	sank	sunk	sinken
sit	sat	sat	sitzen
sleep	slept	slept	schlafen
slide	slid	slid	rutschen, gleiten
smell	smelt, smelled	smelt, smelled	riechen
sow	sowed	sown, sowed	säen
speak	spoke	spoken	sprechen

Irregular Verbs

Infinitive	Simple Past	Past Participle	German
speed	sped, speeded	sped, speeded	rasen, schnell fahren
spend	spent	spent	verbringen, ausgeben
spill	spilt, spilled	spilt, spilled	verschütten
split	split	split	teilen, spalten
stand	stood	stood	stehen
steal	stole	stolen	stehlen
stick	stuck	stuck	kleben, haften
sting	stung	stung	stechen
sweat	sweat, sweated	sweat, sweated	schwitzen
sweep	swept	swept	fegen, kehren
swing	swung	swung	schwingen, schwenken
take	took	taken	nehmen
teach	taught	taught	lehren, unterrichten
tear	tore	torn	zerreißen
tell	told	told	erzählen
think	thought	thought	denken, glauben
throw	threw	thrown	werfen
understand	understood	understood	verstehen
wake	woke, waked	woken, waked	(auf)wecken, aufwachen
wear	wore	worn	tragen (Kleidung)
win	won	won	gewinnen
wind	wound	wound	winden, aufziehen (Uhr)
write	wrote	written	schreiben

Summary of English Tenses

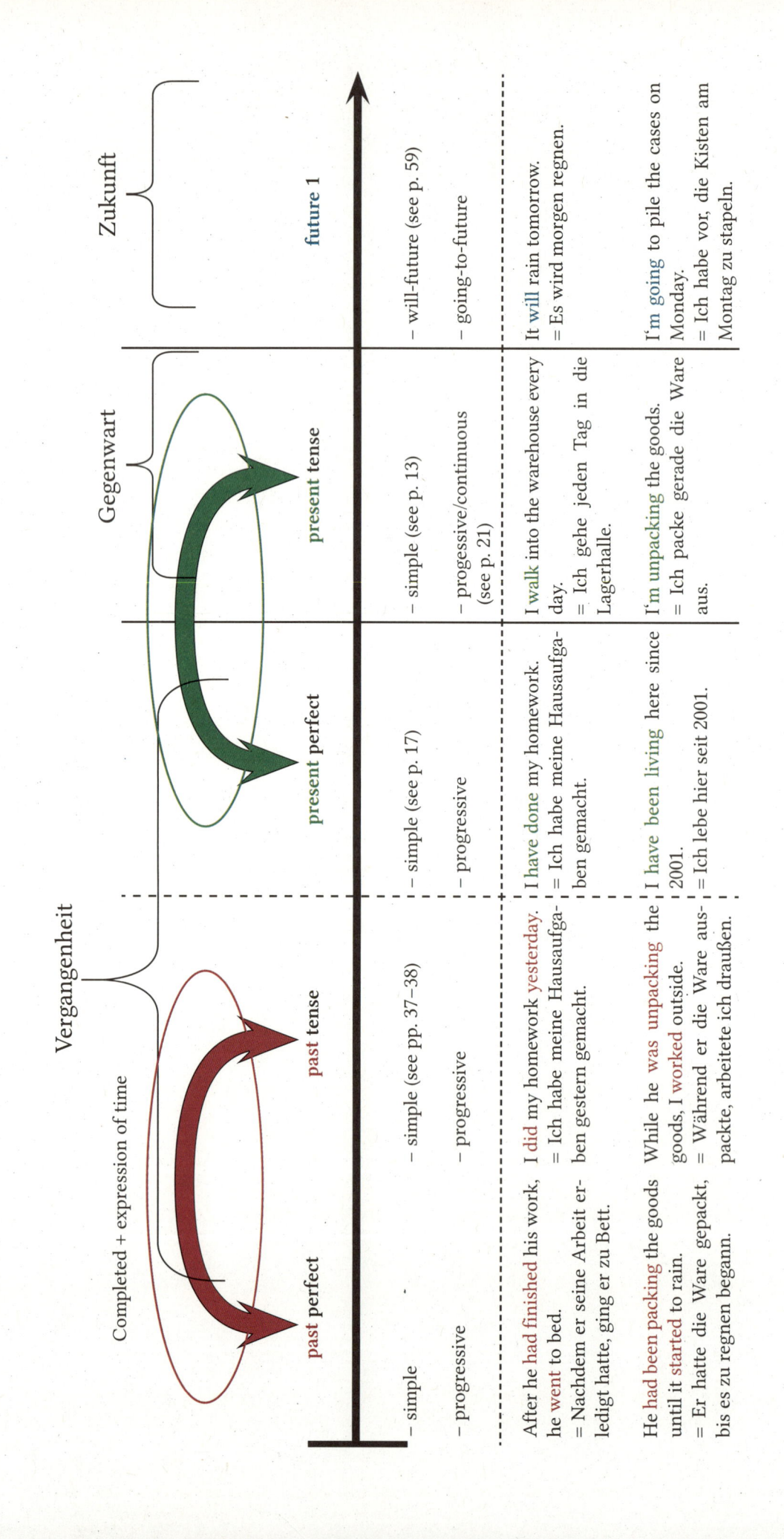

	Vergangenheit		Gegenwart		Zukunft
	Completed + expression of time				
	past perfect	**past tense**	**present perfect**	**present tense**	**future 1**
	– simple	– simple (see pp. 37–38)	– simple (see p. 17)	– simple (see p. 13)	– will-future (see p. 59)
	– progressive	– progressive	– progressive	– progessive/continuous (see p. 21)	– going-to-future
	After he had finished his work, he went to bed. = Nachdem er seine Arbeit erledigt hatte, ging er zu Bett.	I did my homework yesterday. = Ich habe meine Hausaufgaben gestern gemacht.	I have done my homework. = Ich habe meine Hausaufgaben gemacht.	I walk into the warehouse every day. = Ich gehe jeden Tag in die Lagerhalle.	It will rain tomorrow. = Es wird morgen regnen.
	He had been packing the goods until it started to rain. = Er hatte die Ware gepackt, bis es zu regnen begann.	While he was unpacking the goods, I worked outside. = Während er die Ware auspackte, arbeitete ich draußen.	I have been living here since 2001. = Ich lebe hier seit 2001.	I'm unpacking the goods. = Ich packe gerade die Ware aus.	I'm going to pile the cases on Monday. = Ich habe vor, die Kisten am Montag zu stapeln.

Picture Credits

Alamy Stock Photo (RMB), Abingdon/Oxfordshire: { TWHPhotography } 90.5. BC GmbH Verlags- und Medien-, Forschungs- und Beratungsgesellschaft, Ingelheim: 43.1, 43.2, 43.3, 43.4, 43.5, 44.1, 44.2, 44.3, 44.4, 44.5, 44.6, 44.7, 44.8, 44.9, 44.10, 70.1, 70.2, 70.3, 70.4, 70.5, 70.6, 70.7, 70.8, 70.9. Berghahn, Matthias, Bielefeld: 29.1, 29.2, 29.3, 30.1, 54.1, 116.1, 122.5. Beuth Verlag GmbH, Berlin: 65.1, 65.2, 65.3, 66.1, 66.2, 66.3. DIN-Deutsches Institut für Normung e.V., Berlin: 65.4, 66.4. fotolia.com, New York: Marn Wischnewski 87.1; Mikhail Basov 90.4; stockphoto-graf 90.3. iStockphoto.com, Calgary: Hlystov, Pavel 87.6; karlowac 45.8. KBS Industrieelektronik GmbH, Freiburg: 81.3. PantherMedia GmbH (panthermedia.net), München: bobrik74sell 87.5. Ringhut, Daniela, Dreieich: 6.1, 31.1, 49.1, 60.1, 63.1, 66.5, 66.6, 68.1, 68.2, 73.1, 84.1, 84.2, 99.1, 102.1, 107.1, 108.1, 120.1, 123.1, 132.1, 135.1. Shutterstock.com, New York: Aleks822 45.7; AnEduard 46.10; Gorodenkoff 85.4; Loco 45.3; McLittle Stock 46.2; Nejron Photo 81.4; pcruciatti 46.1; Petkovic, Dusan 85.5; Take Photo 45.1; Vasin Lee 46.5; vizual3d 15.1; WAYHOME studio 14.3; YULIYA Shustik 25.1. STILL GmbH, Hamburg: 121.1, 121.2, 121.3, 121.4, 122.1, 122.2, 122.3, 122.4. stock.adobe.com, Dublin: arti om 46.4; blende11.photo 85.3; contrastwerkstatt 14.1; Coprid 46.11; dusanpetkovic1 81.1, 81.2; euthymia 87.3; Fälchle, Jürgen 14.2; Gavluk, Nick 45.9; Globalflyer 87.2; industrieblick 4.1, 85.2; juergenphilipps 85.1; Karnholz, A. 4.5; Kneschke, Robert 4.3; Konstantinos 45.5; Lawrey 46.3; MIGUEL GARCIA SAAVED 45.4; modustollens 45.2; nuttiwut 46.9; patatmac 87.4; Petrik 46.8; pitb_1 46.7; ryszard filipowicz 45.6; showcake 4.4; Spectral-Design 90.6; ThorstenSchmitt 90.1; totenaka 4.2; Worring, Christian-P. 90.2. YPS - York Publishing Solutions Pvt. Ltd.: 31.2, 31.3, 46.6, 119.1, 119.2.